If there was a veil that needed lifting, Karen does it...revealing the deep affection that Jesus has for women. Combining biblical story with her own honest biography, Karen offers a message of hope and dignity to women of all backgrounds.

—Brian Buhler
Retired pastor and spiritual director

Karen relates gritty and raw personal revelations about how God healed the wounds, the self-condemnation, and the hopelessness of a woman who used every means to numb her emptiness, her loneliness, and her lack of hope. Her Scripture references, assigning unique names to God so tenderly in each chapter, and the respective supporting biblical connection makes this book a must-read for anyone struggling with her identity as a woman walking this broken planet. Ending chapters with personal prayers or prayers for her readers, Karen implores women everywhere to say "Yes" to Jesus and embrace the beautiful life they were meant to live. Fully known. Fully loved by their Creator God.

—Theresa Silk
Friend, writer, and artist

I finished Karen's book a couple of days ago and have been soaking in the sweet aroma ever since. I cried, I smiled, I laughed, and I felt her heart from beginning to end. What a gift our Father has given to her to minister to our hearts in her incredible transparency and gentleness, helping us to believe there is hope and that Jesus truly is the answer! Karen nailed it. I loved it all. Her book ministered to me big time, and I know there are going to be many who will be healed and blessed and encouraged to say "yes" to Jesus.

—Lesley Bodenstab
Friend, sister-in-Christ

Karen's raw telling of the story is stunning and sticks with you. There is no pretense here, only riveting authenticity. Get ready for the east-side woman in all of us to meet the Catching God, the Spilling God, or the incredible Singing God. This story meets the longing of my heart to know God deeply. I was delighted to feel ignited in my faith and suddenly motivated to accomplish and create with confidence.

—Chara Presley
Author of *LOVED*

"Dreams rise up at night, huge monstrous things clawing outwards, screaming for escape. Pointing screams and endless evil dreams. Is this normal? These nightmares of turmoil, dark, yelling chaos. Screeching to get out. I don't want to go to sleep. I'm afraid of these dreams..."

An intriguing teaser to Karen Evans' book *Pilgrimage to Beauty*. She tells her story of how God rescued her from a lifetime of meaningless existence. Throughout her stories describing her troubled childhood and growing into adulthood, Karen talks about her loneliness, her struggles, and her desire to want to fit in...to be loved and accepted. Karen poignantly tells how Jesus chased her down for 40 years until He finally "caught her." She beautifully interweaves her stories with stories of women in the Bible and leaves you wanting to hear more from chapter to chapter!

—Alison Plumb
Sister-in-Christ, friend, and fellow writer

Step into true freedom from thoughts of shame, failure, and feeling like you're not enough when reading Karen Evans' new book, *Pilgrimage to Beauty.* Learn how to untie the knots in your heart, as Karen puts it, and receive the true, everlasting love of a Heavenly Father who welcomes you just as you are. Leave behind your defenses, your fear, and your shame as you take this pilgrimage to true beauty found in discovering Jesus. This book is a must-read for all who desire this kind of love and unconditional acceptance.

Krissy Nelson
Author, Speaker, and Host
Krissy Nelson Ministries
krissynelson.com

Pilgrimage to Beauty

Pilgrimage to Beauty

Leaving the Ashes of Your Past for the Beauty of a New Way

KAREN EVANS

CONTENTS

*This book is dedicated to the eastside woman
because a bit of her exists in us all.*

*Therefore, it is dedicated to the women
who are holding this book in their hands,
hoping for a new way.*

ACKNOWLEDGMENTS

To the one and only Jesus Christ, my friend, who called me to write about Him in 2003 so others will know about Him. He waited. He had it all planned out. And then He did the work by dropping all of the stories, verses, scriptures, prayers, poems, parables, and ideas into my heart to be poured out and shared. Surely, none of this book would have been written if He hadn't written it through me. I just had to show up. Thank You for being so patient and gentle with me, my King. Thank You for setting my heart alive for You. Together, we walk this pilgrimage.

To Messenger Books, who came alongside me and helped to unlock the book Jesus prompted me to write: There aren't enough words to express the thanks I have for Jeremiah and Teresa Yancy, Krissy Nelson, and Liz Pitman. Thank you for your inspiring lessons, amazing mentoring, words of encouragement, and God-given wisdom. You've made possible my dream of being a published writer. More to follow. I am forever grateful.

Especially to Teresa Yancy—you got it right away! You knew who I was writing to—the one broken woman out there who needs to hear this message from our Heavenly Father. Your editing gifts beautifully revealed the message in this book, bringing further glory to God in these pages and helping to allure the one to Him. Thank you, dear sister.

To Krissy Nelson, who listened to my many desperate cries when the enemy was striking my mind with millions of doubts and thoughts of "why." You wouldn't have any of it! Instead, you used your voice to send the enemy on his way so I could continue with God's plan to write this book for His Kingdom. Thank you, warrior sister.

To my TASK sisters – Theresa Silk, Alison Plumb and Susan Boland: We sat in a women's church-group meeting one day and put our hands up because "I want to write a book, too!" We began meeting and supporting each other. We talked about our dreams of writing our books. We laughed, slurped tea, ate yummy food and sat in the sunshine. We showed up messy-haired and without make-up at times just to be together. We told each our darkest stories and deepest secrets. We let ourselves be raw and wide open to each other. We cried and confessed. We prayed. Thank you for your kind words of encouragement, your ideas, and your critiques. I am thrilled to be writing books together with friends like you. Your bravery, vulnerability, and beauty astound me.

To Pastor Brian Buhler — You agreed to review my first draft, mostly to confirm it was okay for me to publish your name. But God had another plan! You kindly offered up your precious time and godly wisdom to provide a review of the theological aspects of the manuscript—which I jumped on. I am forever grateful for your gesture. Your suggestions and comments were gentle and wise, bringing glory to our beautiful Jesus. Your contribution to my first book and the difference you have made in spreading the Good News about how much Jesus loves, adores, and values women is tremendous. Thank you, dear brother.

To Chara Presley — You most likely have no idea what an inspiration you have been to me during this season of writing and publishing this book. Our dear friend, Jesus, brought us together through our calling to write and through the Unlocking Your Book ministry. And so we began to meet, virtually, every Tuesday at 10am to share our journey and to pray. Oh, the struggles, tears, prayers, and visions we shared during these precious times. Only He could bring such richness to our Tuesday mornings. He did this in many ways, and one of those ways was through you. Your beautiful faith, loving words, and authentic curiosity and desire to have more and more of God as you journey each moment has encouraged me to want this, too. Thank you, dear sister.

To the one who shouldered most of the burden, my husband Steve, who I've always said is the most beautiful and exciting person I've ever met (besides Jesus!): The right words are inside of me in gratitude, love, and awe, and I struggle to pour them on paper because they won't be enough. I will try. This book took a year to write. For the entire time, you did the most amazing thing—you took over and did most of the cooking, grocery shopping, and housework, along with tending to the yard and walking our happy, jumpy girl, Ruby. You put aside playing your bass (your passionate love) to tend to these things so I wouldn't have to. Thank you, a hundred times over, for reading through the first draft before anybody else and sharing your ideas and wisdom gently but firmly. One gift you have is being able to get the heart of the matter in a nanosecond while it takes me forever. This gift you have shone through brilliantly in your approach to reading and editing my book. Thank you for warming up my cup of tea and putting it at my elbow when my head was so full of words. Thank you for taking me away on nature hikes and beach walks when I needed to get away from the computer screen. Thank you for pushing me through the last few hours when I wanted to give up and walk away. I am forever in your debt. Without you and the loving support you gave to me, there would be no finished book.

"Blessed are those whose strength is in you,
whose hearts are set on pilgrimage."

— Psalm 84:5, NIV —

INTRODUCTION

"Some of us once wandered in the wilderness like desert nomads, with no true direction or dwelling place. Starving, thirsting, staggering, we became desperate and filled with despair. Then we cried out, "Lord, help us! Rescue us!" And he did! He led us right into a place of safety and abundance, a suitable city to dwell in. So lift your hands and thank God for his marvelous kindness and for all his miracles of mercy for those he loves. How he satisfies the souls of thirsty ones and fills the hungry with all that is good!"
— Psalm 107:4-9, TPT —

Can I save myself? Can I do anything lovely or wonderful? Can I do anything whatsoever in this world that is of any significance? Can I be kind even for one full day? On my own, I can't. I tried...or I thought I tried, but did I really? I've lived the life like so many others do: carnally, self-centered. Most of my life, I've lived in the world by taking, not even thinking of giving. I wonder now how I seriously ever thought I'd get away with living that way? How could I do so many drugs, suck back copious amounts of booze, party sick all weekend, and treat others (even ones I say I loved) so ignorantly and poorly? How could I blindly hate myself so much, but still manage to feed myself, pay the rent, and then arrive at a job on Monday morning red-eyed (if I didn't call in sick with some pathetic excuse)? Getting my period was always a handy excuse to use, and who would dare challenge that it always curiously arrived on a Monday? Did I actually think I could go on that way forever? Did I really want to? I wish I hadn't been so self-absorbed and, ironically, so full of self-hatred at the same time.

This is how I lived most of my life. As long as I felt good in the moment and thought I was the prettiest one in the room... Well, life was good then, wasn't it? My thinking was, "Who really gives a hoot about anything and anyone else anyway?" I got high, felt good, had fun (but not really), and the "pressure" was only released until the next time. The pressure of what? Life. I tried to just get through the moment...and all this messiness. This numbing was living. Well, that's what I thought anyway.

"Do you believe in God?"

My mom asked me this question at a time in my life when I was the most distant from her, not wanting to be around her, making her pay for the love she never was able to show me. A single hug would have been good.

I thought, "Heck no. I don't believe in something so terrifying, unbending, and belittling as a Creator of all this mess here on planet earth. Life without God is good, just fine by me 'thank you very much.' Now, go away with your questions about whether I believe in God or not, and leave me to my cleverness."

It seemed so ridiculous to me that she would ask this question; I knew what she'd been through. I thought, "Was God there to help you feed your hungry pack of kids? Was God there when you were beaten up? Was He there when your children died at birth and you got to hold them for only a few minutes as they breathed their last breath? When your new husband hit your boys in the basement and then drank a bottle of whisky to numb his actions, where was your God then? So don't ask me if I believe in that God. *Ha.* Seems like a joke for you to even ask me this." I was so blinded with my pain and my pride.

Of course, I could live without God. Anyone looking at me could see I was doing it just fine. I was working, feeding myself, and living it up in the big city. I was buying a new dress for New Year's Eve and going out with friends and getting drunk. I was dancing to loud music in downtown nightclubs and going home with men. (I even knew some of their names.) All the while, I was still working and providing for myself. Oh, I was filling my empty heart with lots of great stuff: Harvey Wallbangers, cocaine, new shoes, trips to exotic lands—where, guess what, I could drink more alcohol, but now, with the little umbrellas perched atop. (It all seems so sophisticated when there is an umbrella perched.) I could hunt down some drugs there, too. Well, actually, they fell easily into my lap. It's funny how that works—how bad things come so easily. Men came easily, too, much too easily, but the sad thing was I never seemed to get to the good ones (someday). The bad ones are much more interesting, forbidden. The less they liked me, the more I wanted them. "Is this the way of the world or what!" I would think. Yes, apparently.

A few years later, I was in a marriage. In chaos. In destruction. Nothing felt right or good or loving. "If I could only have a baby," I thought. "Then I would have somebody to love, and somebody would love me back." Dreams began to rise up in me at night—huge, monstrous things clawing outward and screaming for escape. Pointing, screaming, and dark jagged limbs roaring towards the other—was this chaos normal? These endless nightmares of turmoil, darkness, and yelling was tormenting me, screeching to get out. I didn't want to go to sleep. I was afraid of these dreams and the darkness within me that they revealed.

Next, I was living in a basement—dark cement walls, spider-webbed ceilings, cluttered junk, and discarded treasures surrounded me. Maybe someday, somebody might need all that stuff, I thought, but not me. I hated that place. This was where I ended up. Alone, broken, with no place to go. This was not home.

In that terrible place, I was the most alone I had ever been, and I was physically sick. In that place, darkness and evil crouched on top of me, licking its hungry, filthy jowls, without a single window to allow the light. This was the closest I'd come to the abyss. "But I can do this thing," I told myself. "I can live again without him. I can crawl out of this dungeon into the blinding, snowy night outside. I can save myself from all this mess... Right? Can't I?"

There is nothing good or freeing about divorce, even when you're the one wanting it so desperately. This is the hard stuff, right up there with cancer. But I told myself that I could do this! They had taught me to rely upon myself, to be independent and strong, to walk it off and, "Stop that crying already!" So, it was in times like that when I was relying completely upon myself—my family is full of strong, tough women—when I was actually the walking dead.

Through all this madness, God never even entered my mind. Not even once. In all this trying to fill the relentless hunger in my gaping, empty, black heart, not once did I think of God. Yet, He was thinking of me. I didn't know this at the time. I wouldn't know of His loving pursuit of me for years.

Ahhh, yes, then there was a glimmer of light. I could see there might be a different way. Did I see it, really? Certainly not clearly, but something did change forty years into my life. Not that I could see a hope of things to come—after all, it's hard to see a straight way when surrounded by darkness. Mysteriously, I was led into a place I didn't want to go. I entered a church building, a place I'd sworn off since childhood. Sadly, as a young girl, the church became a scary place for me. I was frightened one time by the preacher man standing up there, bellowing and pointing his finger at my face, questioning only me, it seemed: "Do you have Jesus in your heart?"

"Hmmm. No. Who's that?" I thought.

You horrible, wretched, fatherless kid, you should be ashamed you don't have Jesus in your heart. This is what my seven-year old brain comprehended, and so I believed this "truth" (lie) for a good, solid four decades. So you see, I personally experienced how the church can sometimes do so much harm with the intention of doing "good." There I was at seven, an undeveloped mind with tender soil for a heart, vowing I would never, after that experience, go back into a church again. I wasn't *it*. I hadn't made it in with the good people, again. I was that filthy, fatherless girl with no hope. Finger-pointing, brimstone-bellowing—it all scared me to death almost. I did not enter again—except for a few weddings and maybe a funeral—for many painful years to come.

When the music started to play in the church that I was mysteriously led into, I began to sing the songs along with everyone else. A sense of peace fell upon me. It seemed as though I had been singing those songs for my entire life. I felt, somehow in a strange way, I had made it home.

This is my Pilgrimage to Beauty.

THE AVAILABLE GOD AND THE BLEEDING WOMAN

"If you knew that God always comes to you…"[1]
— Brother Roger —

"Are you weary, carrying a heavy burden? Then come to me. I will refresh your life, for I am your oasis. Simply join your life with mine. Learn my ways and you'll discover that I'm gentle, humble, easy to please. You will find refreshment and rest in me. For all that I require of you will be pleasant and easy to bear."
— Matthew 11:28-30, TPT —

"I will heal their waywardness. I will love them freely."
— Hosea 14:4, NIV —

THE EASTSIDE WOMAN

We were two of the most unlikely of women to ever meet. There was me, a businesswoman working in a downtown brokerage firm day in and day out, sale after sale, business meeting after business meeting, client expectation after client expectation—talk about stress. And there was you, a druggie, perhaps selling yourself for a hit, addicted to something or everything. You would have stress as well, in a different way, but stress just the same. You didn't have much meat left on your bones, but what was there was tattooed and lean. (It's interesting how drug-addicted women have such well sculpted arms.) You didn't have many teeth left, your blond, stringy hair was matted to your head, and your clothes were worn thin. Your cloth handbag was stained and well-used, most likely holding all you owned, and your sandals were tattered and worn. You were walking towards me on a sunshiny day in the downtown eastside.

Why was I there? I didn't know at the time, but today, I know full well. I was compelled, called, to go down into the sketchy, rough part of the city and walk around to see what might happen. I must have been answering the "God-call" to find a woman who might need to hear from Him because…why else in the world would I be willing to go down *there,* of all places, for a stroll? It was faith.

I remember seeing you and wanting to walk to the other side of the street, over to the safe side, just like the priest who passed over to the other side to avoid the man beaten and robbed in Jesus' story of the Good Samaritan.[2] *Boy, if she asks for money… Well, of course, she is going to ask for money. How can I get out of this?* These were my thoughts. *Stay on this side of the street* was the clear answer I felt in my heart. So I stayed on your side of the street.

You asked me, "Any spare change?" *Of course, I have spare change. I know the money is going towards a bad cause—drug addiction—but if I give her some change, will this help to keep her from turning to a $20.00 sex exchange in a stinking, garbage-strewn, back alley?* These were more of my thoughts.

I chose to give you the money.

"Sure, I have some change. Let me see." I dug into my purse as we walked along the street together and brought out my change purse into the daylight. "Here you go," I said and handed you a dollar or two.

"Do you have any more you can spare? I'm trying to get enough money to stay in a shelter tonight. It costs money to stay there." This may or may not have been true—I didn't know—but it didn't matter what her excuse was because I knew the money was for a different purpose.

"Sure, I think I might have another buck or two here." I handed you some more coins.

You started to talk to me about going to the shelter again and other things, too, but I had trouble understanding what it was you were saying. Then you thanked me for the money. I smiled; you smiled back a toothless grin. Your face was grubby, mascara smudged with days-old makeup, and you smelled of urine. That was okay.

I said to you: "Do you know God loves you?" I didn't know where those words came from or how they were so easily released to you. They simply bubbled up from my heart.

You looked at me like I had a horn growing out of my head. "God loves you," I said again, wondering who was saying these important words so boldly.

We quietly looked into each other's eyes, and then, all at once, we embraced. We hugged each other like long lost friends who'd just found each other again. Slowly, we let go and you stumbled away after another "thank you."

"That was really good what you just said to her."

It was a man's voice. I looked behind me, and there was a man leaning against a handrail at the opening to a building. He had witnessed the whole encounter, but I didn't even know he was there. I don't think you knew he was there either, or maybe you did. It was almost like he was lowered into the scene by an invisible thread. I didn't see him or hear him, and I certainly didn't feel his presence.

"Yeah, that was a really good thing you did for her."

"Oh, gee. But that wasn't really me," was all I could mumble out. Then I walked away, too. I was completely mystified by this experience because this wasn't *me* speaking and hugging. I didn't do that kind of thing; I was (and still am) a private person, generally keeping to myself. But this had happened to me a few times in the past—this speaking out of words when I don't know where they come from and don't have the courage (on my own) to speak them. There was only one possibility: It had to be God. I know this full-well nowadays because everything is possible with God.[3]

To the eastside woman: I hope you met God on that sunshiny day.

SEVEN YEARS LATER

Fast forward about seven years. I never mentioned this experience to anybody, not even to my sweet husband Steve. I hadn't told the story because I didn't want to bring attention to myself, looking for compliments or some sort of a reward. I didn't want to receive any glory at all for that moment; it stayed between God and me. But it really isn't up to me now, is it? If God wants me to tell the story, well…then here it is, the opening story in a book about my journey out of pain into God's love.

I know God was there on the scene that day because, after all, He planned my life way before I was even a thought. And He planned her life, too. By faith, I've prayed for this woman over the years, hoping she made it to a shelter with a seed of God's love planted in her heart. I've hoped that eventually, she said yes to Jesus and began her love journey with God like I did.

Once again, I am compelled and called. This time the calling is to write a book about the topic of shame, overcoming it, gaining freedom from it and untying all the "knots" of shame: worthlessness, insignificance, self-loathing, self-hatred and all those feelings that go into the level of self-esteem that is lower than low. Those feelings must surely be in every woman who has suffered from the trauma of being shamed and unloved as a child in all kinds of ways.

I don't understand addiction to the degree that the eastside woman did—where homelessness, living on the streets, and selling yourself in a back alley for the next fix is normal. I don't understand it, and I haven't lived it, but I have taken enough drugs to know I too was self-medicating, blocking out the feelings, and trying to stop the hurt. I was desperately filling up the black hole and trying to stop the emotional bleed. Tying knot after knot after knot in my heart, protecting its tenderness, hardening it for the battle. What is there to do when you are without hope and the essence of your being feels dirty, grimy, and unlovable? Tie a knot.

THE AVAILABLE GOD

What makes God available to us imperfect, messed up, broken women? Wanting Him, and that's about it. There is nothing fancy about it. It boils down to us wanting to know God. What comes after wanting is seeking. This goes without saying, but I'll say it anyway: We have to *want to* want Him. When we want Him and ask for Him, *instantly,* He is available to us.

> "You will seek me and find me when you seek me with all your heart. I will be found by you," declares the Lord."
>
> — JEREMIAH 29:13-14, NIV

I've heard it a few times, so I might as well share it with you, too: God is a gentleman. This is good to know. He won't be clubbing any of us over the head and dragging us off to eternity if we don't want to be going there. The alternative is horrifying to me, so hopefully, by the end of the book, you'll be wanting and seeking God with all your heart. His approach is a kind and respectful one, just like a gentleman. He wants you to make up your mind about Him, and He's given you exactly what you need to decide—it's called free will, your own choice. Eugenia Price said it this way:

> "God is a gentleman. He is God, but He waits for us to choose to follow Him or to choose our own instincts and wishes. God never pushes Himself upon us. He said so in one of the few passages from the Book of Revelation which I understand: "Behold, I stand at the door and knock." He knocks and waits for us to open our lives to Him."[4]

I am reminded of a story because of a dream I had recently. I woke up in a sweat at 3 a.m. to this whisper: *Not everyone wants to be saved, and not everybody wants to know God.* The story is of a young woman who runs away from home at a young age with a backpack crammed full of her clothes, off to seek freedom from her parents. She ends up in the crack houses located somewhere in the city I live in. Her parents spend days, weeks, and months looking for her. They want to save her and bring her back home where life is better there with her loving family. They never stop looking. When they finally walk into a dilapidated crack house with walls rotting away, steaming with mould and garbage. There were stoned bodies strewn about and in the midst they found her. They were so happy to see their baby daughter, to take her out of that nasty, dark place to a warm, clean, safe home, but she says the unthinkable: "I don't want to go back there. This is my family now; these are my people. You are all dead to me."

What is the alternative to dining at the banqueting table with God throughout eternity once all this mayhem and struggle on earth is over and done with? Well, it's hell. I don't want to go to someplace worse than where I'm at right now—I want to go someplace better. From what I'm reading and understanding from Scripture it sounds like the other option is something worse—really bad—like a sulphur pit. If we opt against being at the banqueting table with God, in the end, that is the alternative.

The Available God is available to us instantly, and the really exciting news is we don't have to jump through hoops, earn brownie points, or climb a flight of steep stairs before He is. Do you know what it is like to try to please everyone at the party, or everyone in your family, or all those supposedly cool "friends"? Do you know what it is like to always wonder how anybody will like you unless you have everything completely and utterly perfect? This is what I used to think and do, but it wasn't just the party; it was pretty much everything in my life.

If you've lived the same way, striving for perfection and trying to please others, you know it's exhausting because it can never be done. There will always be someone who dislikes you or dislikes what you do...like not stacking the dishwasher properly. I'm serious about this, actually. Having a strong streak of the people-pleasing trait because of my upbringing, I admit to seeking approval from family, friends, and acquaintances, especially from a particular woman in my circle of friends, whom I secretly really adored. I wanted so much for her to like me, but I felt whatever I did was never good enough. I just didn't measure up. On one occasion, at a dinner party during the cleanup in the kitchen, I had been stacking dirty dishes into the dishwasher and was about to close it and push the start button when she came around from behind and rearranged the whole thing while saying: "It's shocking how some people just never learned how to load a dishwasher properly." I was crushed. I know it's hard to comprehend something as small as this could cut so deep, but it did, especially to a broken, insecure, and introverted type like me.

Thankfully, Jesus doesn't do this to us. What a relief and what a heap of good news. Instead, He takes us just the way we are—all of our glaring faults, nasty sins, and messy, people-pleasing tendencies combined. I have to keep reminding myself of this truth: He is available, and He is the one dishing out the grace. Nobody else on earth is doing that, so I have asked Him to come on in and help me with my life. Until the time I leave here and join Him on the other shore in eternity, He'll be pouring out grace all over my life. What's this grace thing? It is one of the fundamental ways God shows His love. He gives me favour without my having to prove anything, like how to load a dishwasher perfectly. Grace is His undeserved kindness.

Do you know how much He loves you? He loves me, and he loves you, and actually, it is His sweet desire to love us. I wish I would have known this truth four or five decades ago before all the mayhem started, but I know it now, and I share it with you. The Word says God, the Almighty God, *desires* to love me. All I have to do is say yes and in faith, believe. There is a little bit more to it than just believing, but we'll get to that later, and then you'll see how beautiful He is.

THE BLEEDING WOMAN

There is a wonderful story in the New Testament which has Jesus on the way to the home of an important man in their religious culture. He was surrounded by people on all sides who wanted to be near him. A sick woman was in the crowd, too, that day, although she shouldn't have been. She had been bleeding for twelve years non-stop. I can't imagine living like that; it's bad enough for a week each month but to bleed for twelve years straight—terrible. She was frail and weak, and the only thing to dry up during those twelve, long years was her finances from paying for doctors who couldn't heal her. She lived a life of shame and disgrace because of the religious and social rules of the day; she was considered unclean, and anybody who touched her was unclean as well.

When she heard Jesus was in the vicinity, she took a risk and sneaked into the crowd thinking, *"If I can just touch his clothes, I will be healed"* (Mark 5:28, NIV). What did she have to lose anyway? More shaming and ridicule, more bleeding. She touched Jesus' cloak and was immediately healed. He was immediately *available* to her!

Jesus felt His healing power flow out of Himself, so He asked the crowd: *"Who touched my robe?"* (Mark 5:30, NIV). She confessed to being the one who touched His robe, and He said to her, *"Daughter, your faith has healed you. Go in peace and be freed from your suffering"* (Mark 5:34, NIV). He didn't shame her because she was among the "clean people" when she was considered dirty. He didn't look down upon her and dismiss her; instead, Jesus listened to her story and showed such loving compassion by calling her "daughter." Can you believe it? There is no better name any of us women can hope to be called than *God's Daughter.* In front of a crowd of the "in" people, Jesus restored her health, but He also gave her something just as important: her peace, freedom, and dignity. Oh, Jesus. How can I not love You more and more every day?

TRULY AVAILABLE

A line from a gospel song has been like a sticky note in my head for days now with a particular question replaying over and over: "Why won't you let me love you?" Maybe God is trying to tell me something, or maybe He is nudging me to ask you this very question. He wants to love you, He wants to be in your life, and surely, He is available.

The Bible promises He is available to you, truly available, right up until your very last breath or the final fluttering of your eyelid. He is available to everyone—to me, you, your children, friends, husband, wife, and even to the woman I encountered that day in the downtown eastside... Actually, especially her.

He is available to everyone who says *yes.* It seems to me, He sent me out on a mission that particular day; we were unlikely to ever meet otherwise. He wanted to let the eastside woman know that He loved her. And maybe Jesus was planting a seed into the guy leaning against the handrail watching everything unfold. Perhaps he needed to hear about God's grand love, too.

PRAY

Are you a woman living with feelings of being unloved for way too long now like I was? Maybe you're already curious about God and you want a better life. Ask God to be available to you. He doesn't care about any fancy way of asking Him—a simple desire to know Him is what matters. He has already brought you this far—go all the way into His arms. I've written out a short prayer to help:

> *Dear God, thank You for making Yourself available to me. Thank You that I don't have to be perfect and that You take me just the way I am. I really want to know You, and I want more love in my life. I know the way I am living now isn't working out so well. So please come into my life and love me. Show me another way to live. Thank You that it is Your sweet desire and Your beautiful promise to love me. In faith, I ask You for these things. Amen.*

SOMETHING TO PONDER

What has stopped you in the past from looking into the availability of God in your life? If you knew He is available to you always, would you seek Him? Would you let Him love you?

THE RESCUING GOD AND THE WOMAN AT THE WELL

"Turn your ear to me, come quickly to my rescue."
— Psalm 31:2, NIV —

"His love broke open the way and he brought me into a beautiful broad place. He rescued me – because he delights in me!"
— Psalm 18:19, TPT —

NOBODY LOVES ME

I was a toddler who teeter-tottered back and forth on my feet chanting, "Nobody loves me. Nobody loves me. Nobody loves me." I *became* this lie. How heartbreaking this must have been for a mother to watch her child rocking back and forth in the backyard, chanting these words. I remember a male cousin ridiculing me for these actions relentlessly. How ashamed I was for acting this way. I couldn't help myself though; I was tying tight knots in my heart during those days, folding into myself and withdrawing. The chanting and rocking were my coping mechanisms for my early belief system that nobody loved me.

MY SHAME GLASSES ON

God dropped this in my heart one day:

> *I want you to write about shame. You grew up feeling shamed. You felt guilty stopping a car when you wanted to walk in a crosswalk to get to the other side of the street. You believed it was okay for others to call you names and label you with lies. You thought you were never good enough. This thought was the reason you did so many of the things you did—it was your reaction to being shamed. You folded into being a small person without a voice and not being heard, instead of my beautiful daughter. You experienced shame like many women do, but you have overcome it by knowing Me. This is what I want you to write about because so many of my dear daughters are bound with shame, not living the beautiful lives they could be living. I want my daughters to know I adore, love, and value them.*

If I could take one thing out of my past and kick its ugly butt down into the abyss, it would be shame. Shame belittles and humiliates. Shame is a strong connector to the false values each woman has of herself, and if someone is shamed every day, then they feel they have become little and irrelevant. I don't even want to write about it, to travel backwards down that jagged road. I don't want to stoop down and pull on those dirty, worn-out, old shoes and feel again the pain of those stinging blisters scraping at my heart again, but God has asked me to. His ways are always for the good, so this is the best reason of all to write about shame and its consequences.

Why did I carry so much shame and guilt from my childhood? As a young woman, I used to walk across the streets in the downtown city where I lived and feel guilty for being in the crosswalk stopping a car and its driver from making a left-hand turn. Yes. I felt guilty for crossing the street. I know this sounds ludicrous, but this is how I navigated life. If I was feeling guilty for walking across the street, what other dysfunctional things was I doing from the position of feeling shamed and unloved? Could it be that my whole life was lived from one big shame pit? Could it be that everything I said and did was viewed through shame glasses? Good things—shame view. Bad things —shame view. How in the world could I ever get out of that mess? How could I possibly look forward with any sense of hope, excitement, glee, or joy when I was viewing everything with those glasses on?

Where did my shame come from, and why did it penetrate so deeply for me? I know this sounds like a cliché but I didn't understand why I couldn't simply let it roll off of me like the water off a duck's back.

THE SENSITIVE KIDS

I was one of those little girls growing up who cried at stuff like the ending to the Old Yeller movie and then was teased for it. They said I was soft-hearted. I was talked about like there was a bad smell hanging around me, like I was some sort of weirdo amongst a pack of normal, sweet-smelling, strong-hearted kids who never cried. The words spoken about me sounded like I was doing something terribly wrong. "How could I be doing something wrong?" I would think. "I was crying about Old Yeller dying and who doesn't cry when dogs die?"

The people who were my "gods" at the time, the grown-ups, said I was shy.

Shy.

Shy.

Shy.

This was my label. It was almost dismissive in a sense. "Oh, ignore her, she's shy." So I became that label—a shy-baby, cry-baby, who didn't say much—in order to keep them happy and keep me safe.

Were you one? One of the highly sensitive kids. Everything seemed so much more intensified being a sensitive one. Harsh words were far more devastating to me than a beating with a broom handle. Did you feel ashamed of yourself growing up like I did? Did you feel unloved, too? I did. And to make childhood even more dangerous, I was in a family who didn't show emotions, affection, or talk much. I learned early on in life to fold into myself, withdraw, protect my heart – I wasn't going to let them hurt me again – especially the scary ones. I'm not writing to gain sympathy but to tell the good news of it all, the beautiful life that happened for me eventually; how I tied knots in my heart for protection, the folding into myself and then the folding back out – how God untied those same knots and set me free.

THE WOMAN AT THE WELL

I have been reading the story about Jesus' encounter with the woman at the well to see if there could be a connection between her story two thousand years ago and my story. I want there to be a connection. I want Jesus to be just as passionate for me as He was for the women He met on earth, so I'm pouring over stories of these women from the Bible, paying attention to His reaction to them—how He validated and loved them and how He blessed each one.

It was around noon when a woman with a water jug on her hip walked up to the communal well on the outskirts of town to draw water from it. Nobody else from the village was there—the other women had come and gone, avoiding the heat of the day. This woman was avoiding them. She was an outcast; otherwise, she would have strolled up there with those same women. She was setting her jug down on the ground when she saw a Jewish man sitting on the edge of the well, resting.

"Will you give me a drink?"

— JOHN 4:7, NIV

It was Jesus of course. Men ignored women back then; they didn't waste their breath talking to any of them...but Jesus did. This act alone shows how much He loves women. This woman mattered to Jesus. He had sent His disciples into the village to get food, leaving Him alone at the well. Do you think He did this on purpose so He would have a quiet encounter with her? If God knows every single hair on my head, and has numbered all my days, then He knew this woman was on her way up to the well that afternoon. Oh, The Rescuing God.

"Why would a Jewish man ask a Samaritan woman for a drink of water?"

— JOHN 4:9, TPT

She was surprised He spoke to her at all, so she took the time to remind Him that Jews and Samaritans were at odds with each other, foreign enemies.

"Jesus replied, "If you only knew who I am and the gift that God wants to give you—you'd ask me for a drink, and I would give to you living water."

— JOHN 4:10, TPT

She thought this was an odd reply so she asked Him how in the world He was going to draw water from such a deep well when He didn't have the bucket or a cup to do it.

"But those who drink the water I give will never be thirsty again. It becomes a fresh, bubbling spring within them, giving them eternal life."

— JOHN 4:14 NLT

Then she asked Jesus how she could get the water He was talking about so she wouldn't have to keep coming to the well every day. She didn't get it, and honestly, I didn't get Him at first, either. I didn't know there was a God who would actually rescue me from my own self-made craziness so I wouldn't have to keep searching for all the wrong things to help me feel better.

Did you notice that there were two conversations going on at the well? She was talking about the physical, and Jesus is talking of the spiritual; she's talking about well water, and He's talking about spiritual, living water; she's talking about getting out of having to trudge up to the well every day, while He's talking about giving her His love.

How did Jesus rescue this woman? He told her to go get her husband and come back, but she replied that she had no husband.

> *"That's true," Jesus said, "for you've been married five times and now you're living with a man who is not your husband. You have told the truth."*
>
> — JOHN 4:17B-18, TPT

It wasn't cool during Jesus' time for a woman to have more than three husbands in a lifetime. Having multiple husbands brought about religious disapproval and most certainly cultural shaming.[1] Evidently, she had gone from man to man, searching and hoping... *Maybe this next guy will make me feel better about myself. Maybe this man will love me.* She was coping as best she could on the outside, but Jesus knew how messed up she was on the inside—where it mattered the most.

She immediately complimented Jesus saying, *"You must be a prophet!"* (John 4:19, TPT). She doesn't let him answer but goes on to discuss the differences between how her people and His people worship in different ways. This is something I would do—deflect the intimacy by changing the subject. Who wants to talk about failed relationship issues?

She didn't want to face her own issues, so perhaps she thought some banter would redirect Him away from her moral and spiritual dilemma. It didn't work. Jesus explained to her that someday soon, she was going to have to make a choice and do what's right, but she deflected again and pointed out that when the Messiah came, he would explain all this confusing stuff to everybody.

> *Jesus said to her, "You don't have to wait any longer, the Anointed One is here speaking with you—I am the One you're looking for."*
>
> — JOHN 4:26, TPT

Your Rescuing God is here.

I believe it must have been His eyes. When she looked into them while He spoke, I'm sure she saw something different from any eyes she'd ever looked into before. She knew at that moment that this man was The Rescuing God, The Messiah. She left her empty jug there at the well with Him and ran into the village to tell the others. It is interesting to notice she left her jug there with Him. Is she asking Him to wait for her? Perhaps hinting, "Oh, please don't leave, I'll be right back."

He knew her completely—from her misguided strategy in looking for love, to the unsatisfactory validation she never received—He knew her deep, dirty secrets of the six men she'd had in her life...and He still loved her without limits.

He conveyed to the woman at the well: *You need to stop looking for fulfilment in everybody and anybody and find it only in Me.* He gave her the option of another way, a better way.

Jesus announced to a woman *first* that He was the Messiah. Not just any woman, but this woman at the well, who was essentially a foreign enemy to the Jewish people. He placed so much value on this woman that even as a foreign enemy to the culture He was born into, He wanted to save her and bring her into eternity with God. He wanted her to know, *I am here to rescue you and all you have to do is say yes.* And she did. She left her jug (and her old life) with Him and ran to announce to the whole village, "The Messiah is here!"

FATHERLESS ME

The first sweep of shame came when I was abandoned by my dad. Actually, he didn't do the initial abandonment part. In fact, it was my mom who took us away. He just never ever came by to visit us.

It was 1959. She took my brother, sister, and I and ran. He was an alcoholic already and had begun to physically abuse her. She left. Smart woman—women didn't do that in 1959. They didn't grab their kids with nothing but the clothes on their backs and flee their husbands. It seems the women back then just sucked it up, no matter how ugly and dangerous the environment was. I remember her recounting to me in her later years about her decision to leave: "Either I joined in with the drinking and the abuse or I got out."

I am thankful she did. But… (There is always a but, isn't there?) I grew up without a dad, so I spent the most formative years of life without one. This manifested for me into not feeling loved, stunted emotions, and being unable to connect intimately—the typical outcomes of being a fatherless daughter.

It's a big deal for daughters to lose their dads, but for me, I don't remember any of it. It's a blank wall, an expansive desert landscape with nothing but cracked dried ground. A huge missing piece of me. *A daddy to protect me? There is supposed to be somebody who actually does that? A man in the family who lives with us—loves, protects and adores us? Really?*

So you see, when spiritual people, Christian or otherwise, with good intentions, try to compare the love received from a Heavenly Father with the love we received from our earthly fathers, I get worked up. Why? Because I've heard something like this said many times: "You know how wonderful it is to be loved by your own dad—well, just imagine that love being magnified, and that's what the love of a Heavenly Father is like." But some of us didn't experience any love from our earthly dads. Some of us were abused by our dads. Some of us were made to feel insignificant and unworthy. What if your dad wasn't there at all, like mine? How can you equate or compare nothing with something?

How can a fatherless daughter feel any protection when the protector isn't there? How can she even begin to feel any validation or love when the "love her" validator is completely absent? Why wasn't I love-able? What was wrong with me that my dad didn't want me? Why didn't he fight for me? He never came to visit and he never came back to rescue me. The only time I felt comfort was in bed at night as I curled into the fetal position, rocking myself to sleep.

SHAME IN THE SCHOOLYARD

Other girls at school had the love of their dads. Not me. It was and is a missing piece of my life. Every girl wants her father's affection and approval. When my women friends talk of their fathers in such loving ways, all I can do is nod my head, smile and say: "Yeah, right." I have no idea what they are talking about. Blank. Nothing. One of my sweet girlfriends, Carolyn, loves spending time with her dad, just the two of them without her mom around sharing a simple evening of playing a card game or watching a football game.

That seems lovely enough, except I don't get it. (Plus, I don't like football.)

I'm not jealous or envious at all—it's just a nothingness, a void. I've heard and read that the relationship between father and daughter is a special one, even crucial to the positive emotional development of a girl in almost all aspects of her life.

Hmm, that might explain a lot.

One day, I was walking home from elementary school with my friend, Marianne. We were all walking home with our friends back then, so please don't be too shocked. Our moms didn't pick us up after school to drive us back home. On the first day of school, we were shown the way to get to school and back, and then we were left to our own devices, dodging jeers from the popular kids and shoves from the bullies. So, here we were, navigating our way home, when she asked me this question:

"I heard you don't have a father. Is that true? You don't have a dad?"

"No." I said.

"How come? Where is he?" I couldn't answer her because I had no idea where he was or who he was.

"But why don't you have one?" I couldn't answer this question either and wasn't savvy enough yet to come up with a little white lie so she would still like me.

I felt ashamed and humiliated as I walked up the road to my house, having left Marianne at the corner to go to hers. My thoughts were dismal... *And, now, the whole school will find out about my hidden secret: I am a poor, fatherless kid.*

I felt like an outcast, different from all the other kids at school. In the mid 1960's, everyone had a dad in their house. Even if he was a big, nasty, mean one, he was still there. Was a mean one better than no dad at all? On that particular day, I would have picked having a mean one.

The shame and humiliation didn't come just from the ones who held power over us (parents, teachers, pastors, and all the grownups we knew); it came, innocently enough I suppose, from our classmates as we walked home from school.

TYING KNOTS

The heart is where our tenderness lies and where our emotions bleed, so I tied knots in my heart to stop the bleeding and to guard myself against hurt. After all, I didn't see anybody else protecting me. I thought if I cried, nobody would love me. Heck, I thought nobody would even *like* me. And, heaven forbid, if I said the wrong thing, they *surely* wouldn't love me. I quickly learned that the best way to please anybody was to keep quiet, shove the feelings down deep, and lie as best I could to avoid any conflict and to keep them all pleased with me. *But if I tied up my heart to keep the pain out, did I actually keep the love out, too?*

At my house, we didn't touch or hug much. The touching I witnessed was hitting and slapping in the homes, neighbourhoods, schools, and backyards. I certainly didn't want any part of that kind of touching. The first hug I remember from my own mom was when I was around fourteen years old, and I had already been experimenting with drinking. I had spent the night with a girlfriend in town, where we managed to convince somebody to get us six beers, and we drank them with a couple of boys across the train tracks in the mill yard. We didn't need more than a few bottles to get us drunk, acting silly and feeling free—we thought that was so much fun.

Mom picked me up from my friend's house the next day, and I was feeling rather poorly, hungover after my two bottles of beer. We drove back to the farm in silence and walked up the stairs into the farmhouse, but at the top of the stairs, she turned around and hugged me. I wasn't that clever, so she probably knew exactly what I had been up to the night before. Perhaps her heart was breaking as I was already showing signs of heading down a path of destruction at fourteen.

MORE ABOUT FATHERLESS DAUGHTERS

I'm uncomfortable with the huggy, kissy, feely thing—a result of not experiencing much affection from a mom or a dad. Instead, I pursued affection and attention in troubling ways. I recklessly went about looking for anyone...anything...to just *please* love me. Well, you can imagine the mess I created for myself, not to mention a failed marriage full of alcohol, drugs, deception, and adultery. My life was a circle of craziness, wondering: *How in the world am I ever going to get out of this alive?*

How do children and teenagers cope, set boundaries, or feel secure when there is no affection or love being shown to them and no guidance given? They become like what I became. Shut up. Silent. People-pleasers. Needing approval from anyone.

The book, *The Fatherless Daughter Project*,[2] helped me to understand some of the tragic ways in which women deal with being abandoned by their father, or, as in my case, not having one in the first place. The authors, Babul and Luise, surveyed over five thousand fatherless women for their book and discovered some interesting facts on the coping mechanisms used by these women. Here are the top ten methods:

- Isolation 41%
- Sexual promiscuity 33%
- Alcohol 30%
- Suicidal thoughts 24%
- Food 28%
- Illegal drugs 19%
- Shopping 16%
- Running away from home 12%
- Anorexia/bulimia 11%
- Internet 11%

These are some of the things I used, too—I could be a poster child for fatherless daughters.

I received some guidance from a counsellor once, who explained to me that there was evidence I had received love and affection in my childhood. She told me that otherwise, I would have become a completely different person. I think she meant I would be a really, *really* bad person because I was messed up, and she knew all about my issues. Did she mean I would have ended up walking the streets and back alleys like the eastside woman or worse? I may have been better off than others, but I still felt so sad and empty inside.

THE RESCUING GOD

I need confidence that I am loved and that I matter to somebody. I need a God to wrap His arms around my broken, weary heart and tell me I'm adored and special. I don't need anything fancy, just a wrapping of loving arms and a reassuring whisper: *"You are my daughter, and I love you. With me you are safe and protected, and I will never abandon you."*

It's as simple as that. I need a Rescuing God. Do you?

> *"The LORD is close to the broken hearted; he rescues those whose spirits are crushed."*
>
> — PSALM 34:18, NLT

Thank God, He rescues us from ourselves. He touches our hearts with *Himself,* looks into our eyes, and says: *I will rescue you. I have just the thing you need: My love, which is ready to be poured into your knotted-up heart. I will loosen the places too tight for love to flow through. Have faith in Me, your Rescuing God, and you will find rest for your weary soul.*

Will you let Jesus love you? It takes a leap of faith. I know. It takes being vulnerable. I know that, too. And it takes some measure of confidence in God that when you cry out to be rescued, He will rescue you.

TRULY RESCUING

I know God rescued me from my self-made chaos, so even today, I want to thank Him for it with prayers like this one:

> *"Oh, Lord, how I need You. Every minute of every day, I need You. Thank You that You rescued me out of my mess. Thank You, Jesus, that You have provided everything for me and You always will: salvation, love, goodness, kindness, rest and peace, a loving and*

beautiful husband, an amazing place to live my one remarkable life,
sweet family, and beautiful friends (old and new). Even more, You
have provided me with every strawberry I've ever popped into my
mouth, every sip of tea, every flower ever to appear in my island
garden, every pair of shoes I walk the roads with You in, and every
breath I take. And I don't deserve any of these blessings because of all
the things I've done in my past. Thank You, Jesus, You will rescue me
again and again because I am Your daughter, and I know You will
never abandon me. Amen."

PRAY

Your prayer to Jesus doesn't have to be fancy. He just wants you to let
Him love you, so a simple prayer is all He is waiting for—something
like this:

"Jesus, please save me from myself. Rescue me from the messes I've
created. I am sorry for all of it, and I want to leave it all behind like
the woman at the well that You helped. I want to change the way I am
living. Please help me, Jesus, to live the life You have especially
planned for me all along. I want to know You. Thank You. Amen."

Then wait to see what He does. Have faith, and expect Him to move.

"From his temple he heard my voice; my cry came before him, into his ears."

— PSALM 18:6, NIV

SOMETHING TO PONDER

Is there something in your life you want to be rescued from? I needed
a God who could rescue me from myself and save me. Do you?

THE UNFAILING GOD AND THE
SLEEPING DAUGHTER

"Love never fails."
— 1 Corinthians 13:8, NIV —

"Your love, Lord, reaches to the heavens, your faithfulness to the skies.
Your righteousness is like the highest mountains, your justice like the
great deep. You, Lord, preserve both people and animals. How
priceless is your unfailing love, O God!"
— Psalm 36:5-7, NIV —

I am putting my faith in The Unfailing God. He is unfailing because He never fails to love us. Even in the days when we don't want Him near and when it is impossible to believe there is anybody who really cares about us anyway, there He is. Sadly, when you are a young girl (as I was) and have just had a terrible experience of being shamed in a church (as I did), why would you want God? I didn't.

Surely, I didn't want that God.

SHAME AT CHURCH

"Those who look to him are radiant, their faces are never covered with shame."

— PSALM 34:5, NIV

I used to believe I was covered in shame. It's what the grownups said about me: *"You must be ashamed of yourself."* Was I? I felt I was because they told me so, and what did I know? I was a kid, and they were the gods. Nobody was teaching me about right and wrong or guiding me through what the consequences might be with my right or wrong choices. Instead, when I did something wrong, I was reprimanded with, *"You should be ashamed of yourself."* It seemed to be the way the world taught its children back in those days. Maybe it still does. If it wasn't the strap or the belt, it was the shame.

Unfortunately, teaching with shame didn't work so well for the sensitive children. In fact, it devastated us, and I suspect lasted longer and tied up more knots in our hearts than any spanking ever did. I wasn't on the end of the belt too often, but I was on the receiving end of the tongue's bittersweet shame words, so I know the results of it well enough.

One of the most devastating shaming "lessons" I received was in a church when I was seven years old. One of my schoolmates asked me if I would like to go to catechism classes with her. I didn't have a clue what catechism classes were, but I knew my friend took them, her family went to church, and they were one of the "popular" families in the small town I grew up in, so of course, I wanted to go. *"If I go, will she like me even more?"* I wondered.

The Sunday arrived when I would be joining my friend for the classes. I didn't have Sunday clothes because we weren't church-goers, but my mom did the best she could. I wore the dreaded, pleated, navy-blue school jumper, white blouse, and those ugly, sensible saddle oxford shoes (the horror of every little girl forced to wear them).

Oh, I just figured out the root of my love of shoes.

I walked down to the church on my own and met up with my girlfriend there. We sat in the pew with the adults while the preacher talked words I didn't understand. He was like the teacher in Charlie Brown cartoons— "Wah, wah, wah, wah." There was singing, page turning, and passing around a basket. I didn't understand any of it, but I was happy to be with my friend and keen for the catechism class to begin.

Then it happened. The incident which shamed me out of any church for the next thirty-five years. The preacher was above me on the platform when he turned towards me and pointed his finger directly at my face and asked:

"Do you have Jesus in your heart?"

Okay... so who is Jesus? I had no idea what he was talking about. He repeated the question again, this time with a much sterner face and louder voice, finger still pointing at my innocent, now blushing, face.

"Do you have Jesus in your heart?"

Why was he pointing at me in front of the whole church and my favourite friend? Why me? I didn't have Jesus in my heart. Nobody had explained who this Jesus person was only that He should be in my heart. He wasn't there as far as I could tell, and how would He get in my heart in the first place? I was terribly confused. I was being yelled at in front of the whole church for what I had or hadn't done to get this Jesus person into my heart. My heart heard the unspoken accusation: "And shame on you for Him not being there."

I don't recall what happened next, but spiritually, I can tell you exactly what happened: I never went back into a church again. I felt ashamed I wasn't like everyone else sitting in the pews. I vowed to stay out of those places for good, and I managed to do this for three solid decades.

It was a demeaning, shameful, and frightening experience. The preacher thought he was doing the right thing by shouting out this question, but it had the opposite effect on me. It terrified and humiliated me.

I thought to myself, *"What is wrong with me that I didn't know who this Jesus person is, and why isn't He in my heart when He seemed to be in everybody else's? Am I so dirty, ugly and unlovable Jesus doesn't want me either?"* Tie a knot.

I made a vow to stay away from church forever. I rejected God. When we say no to God, does it cause Him to look the other way and never have anything to do with us again, or does our "no" break His heart? I believe it saddens Him, but He never lets us go because, after all, we are His creation.

Does He keep His eye on us? Does God say, "When she finally gets her act together and returns to Me, well, maybe then I will listen to her. Maybe I'll save her then"? Is He like that? I don't think He is. Here's His promise:

> *"For I know the plans I have for you,' says the Lord. 'They are plans for good and not for disaster, to give you a future and a hope.'"*
>
> — JEREMIAH 29:11, NLT

THE SLEEPING DAUGHTER

She was the daughter of one of the most popular men in town—a ruler in the synagogue. Her father had power, which means she was from the good side of town. She was protected, loved, and cared for. Even with all his connections, Jairus pleads with Jesus, *"My little daughter is dying. Please come and put your hands on her and so that she will be healed and live"* (Mark 5:23, NIV).

By this time, Jairus has heard all the stories about Jesus and perhaps witnessed some of the healing miracles He was doing around the Galilean countryside. Did Jairus already believe Jesus was the Messiah they were all so desperately waiting for, or was he responding to Jesus' reputation only as a great healer? Whatever he believed, Jesus heard Jairus' plea and agreed to go and help his daughter.

However, there was a delay along the way. As Jesus walked through a throng of people, a woman suffering twelve long years from chronic, internal bleeding touched His robe, and she was immediately healed. Jesus felt power leave Him and stopped to find out who had touched His hem. When she finally stepped up to confess, Jesus had a conversation with her. He paused to hear her story, and then He blessed her with peace and freedom from her affliction.

Amidst all this, a messenger arrived, coming straight from Jairus' house with a message for him.

> *"There's no need to trouble the master any longer—your daughter has died."*

> — MARK 5:35, TPT

In spite of this disheartening news, Jesus encouraged Jairus to not give into his fears and just believe. When they arrived at Jairus' house, there was quite a commotion going on. Loud wailing and crying were underway for the little girl thought to be dead. As I read this part of the story, it makes me wonder how many times we discard a woman before she has had a chance to bloom. How often does our culture dismiss women who we think are dead already? *There's no helping her. Well, there's nothing I can do—she's a druggie, a hooker, a loser, a drunk.*

An exchange took place between Jesus and the wailers. Upon entering the home, Jesus said to them, *"Why all this grief and weeping? Don't you know the girl is not dead but merely asleep?"* (Mark 5:39, TPT). The wailers had a good chuckle at Jesus, probably rolling their eyes because they did this for a living. They were hired to wail and mourn at funerals, so they were quite confident she was dead. What happened next is funny to me. Jesus put them all out of the house. *There's the door—off you go.* He cleared the house, and those people missed out on one of the biggest events to ever happen in that town's history. During His time on earth, Jesus brought three people back to life; Jairus' daughter was one of them.

Jesus took Jairus and his wife into the girl's room along with three of His disciples. She was lying on her bed and was dead, apparently. He gently took hold of her hand and said the sweetest thing ever: *"Little girl, wake up from the sleep of death"* (Mark 5:41, TPT).

Scripture says her spirit returned to her, and she immediately got up and walked around the room. She was alive again! Her parents were stunned. Their sweet, twelve-year old daughter had died! They thought they wouldn't see her again, watch her get married, or have grandchildren through her. All their dreams were shattered until Jesus called the girl's spirit back to her, and she opened her eyes and breathed again. Hallelujah! Jairus and his wife would see their daughter get married and they will meet their grandchildren one day. Everyone in the room was flabbergasted over the miracle, but our wonderful Jesus brought them all back down to earth by telling her parents to *"give her something to eat"* (Mark 5:43, TPT).

I love the phrase He used, *"little girl,"* because I discovered during my study of this encounter, it suggests Jesus spoke with the same tone and affection that you and I would use if we were saying, "Oh, you little lamb."[1] Isn't this beautiful? He took her hand and called her His little lamb. He is the Good Shepherd, and she was one of His little lambs.

The miracle of Jairus' daughter is a beautiful story of coming alive in Jesus. It is not unlike my own story, only it took me forty years to come alive with Him. He tried many times to get my attention. God didn't make any sense to me. I was confused about Him, and sadly, after my frightening church experience, I was also afraid of Him.

SCRUBBING WALLS

I was ten years old when I lost my sister. Our family lived in a little house on a hill, where my sister and I shared the same bed in a tiny bedroom. My brothers shared the other bedroom, and Mom slept on a pullout couch in the living room. This was the life of a single mom with five kids in the late 1960s in rural Canada.

My sister and I also shared chores, and when we were done, we shared outdoor games and adventures. She landed a babysitting gig, and we even shared this—but most likely, I went along just to keep her company or so that I wouldn't be home alone at night while our mom worked.

One of my sweetest memories of our time together as young sisters was watching the Miss America pageant on TV while we babysat. We didn't have a television set at our house yet, and when we finally got one, it was black and white and the size of a box of Captain Crunch cereal, so we got the thrill of a big colour TV whenever we babysat. I loved the Miss America pageant, always hoping for Miss California, blonde and tanned, to be crowned. We had cousins who lived there, so this was another reason for casting my vote for California. Our neighbour invited us down to watch the pageant on Saturday nights even when she didn't need our babysitting services. With a bag of potato chips and a bottle of Pepsi, we plopped in front of her TV and glued our eyes to the screen "oohing and aahing" over the swimsuit competition and the silky gowns during the first and final walk. We hung on every word the contestants spoke about how she was going to change the world if she wore the crown.

The times were changing in our little town. The hippies had moved in, coffee houses had opened up in church basements, hair was getting longer on boys and skirts shorter on girls, peace signs were painted on road signs, and amazing music was blasting onto the scene everywhere: The Beatles, Carol King, Elton John, The Rolling Stones, The Guess Who, Jim Croce, and so on. Teenagers were starting to protest and break away from the establishment, which was basically their parents. My sister was in the middle of it all, a social butterfly, and one of the most popular girls at our school. At least, that is how I saw her. My heart was bursting with love for her, and my eyes were always admiring her. While I was this skinny, pencil-thin, knobby-kneed girl, she was a voluptuous, outgoing, vivacious, and popular young lady. She was never without a boyfriend if she wanted one.

It was in the midst of this tumultuous background when I lost her. She was sent away to live with our dad, who lived in another province, where she would finish the rest of her schooling. It's still a mystery to me why she was sent away to live with him. I came home from school one cold, winter day and was told she was being driven into town that very moment to the depot where she would be catching the Greyhound bus to Alberta. Our closet with the broken door was missing her clothes, and her little jewellery box and shoes were gone; I didn't see her again for several years. She was gone, and the tragedy of the loss was worsened because we didn't get to hug and say good-bye to each other. I did the only thing I knew how to do. I grabbed a bucket and a rag and scrubbed the walls of the bathroom while I cried my heart into broken pieces. I scrubbed the walls until I fell to the floor exhausted and completely cried out. I had lost my sister, the one I adored and loved, the one who loved me back, the one I shared all my secrets with. My only sister was gone and along with her, any security that I was safe and loved. This loss added to the empty feeling that was already growing inside me.

> *"Send your kind mercy-kiss to comfort me, your servant, just like you promised you would. Love me tenderly so I can go on, for I delight in your life-giving truth."*
>
> — PSALM 119:76-77, TPT

THE KNOTS IN OUR HEART

When I think of the inside of a heart, I think of soft, bluish-pink, tubular vessels. I think of pliable vents and soft valves opening, closing, and pumping. I think of life flowing. But should there be a knot inside of all this delicate intricacy, the life blood would stop flowing freely.

Of course, life doesn't end with a single knot. However, if you get many knots in your heart and soul, life isn't as lovely as it could be. Maybe the knots get brittle. Perhaps the knots grow as blood flows around and pain sticks to it, one hurt at a time, until soon, you have a bigger knot. Some part of you never intended for this knot to get so big, but another part of you did. You really don't know the knot is there, you just tied it there to help stop the bleeding from a harsh word about your face, your voice, your skinny legs, or the well-used line, "You should be ashamed of yourself."

I've noticed over the years, during all of my emotional traumas, I always do the same thing to cope—I scrub stuff. I guess it's good in the sense I get my housework done, but not good when it comes to dealing with the empty feeling inside, shame, rejection, and the deep hurt. Is there a way that you deal with the emptiness and pain deep inside your soul? Do you scrub the house spotless? Drink the bottle to its last drop? Cut yourself to release the pain? Pick somebody up for random sex? Eat a quart of ice cream? These avenues of false comfort seem like an unsatisfying and dangerous place to live. There is another way to be comforted from the agony of loss, rejection, abuse, shame, and feeling you are unloved.

THE UNFAILING GOD

"Let the dawning day bring me revelation of your tender, unfailing love."

— PSALM 143:8A, TPT

Most of my life I've believed the lie that nobody was looking out for me, let alone loving me. Could the opposite be true—that God saw it all and said it was good? After all, He's the one who put the divine plan in place for my life, so would this dramatic event be beneficial to His loving plan or hinder it?

I believe Jesus, who dragged me out of the muddy murky pit, has been there all along in my life even when I didn't know who He was.

The Unfailing God never fails to love me, never fails to protect me, never fails to hold my hand and lead me into a beautiful life. True, I had a troubled life ahead of me and heartache to endure while living a life as if God didn't exist. Quite honestly, I'd prefer to let all the messiness of those years stay buried instead of having to revisit them and grab the nuggets to write it all down. But I must, you see, because if I don't, the whole story of how beautiful and loving He is won't be shared with you. All the time I was sleeping (unaware of Him), He was never unaware of me. He never walked away from me. He never turned his back on me even though I had turned my back on Him. I now put my faith into the promise that God has been looking after me since the beginning. The Unfailing God.

"The faithful love of the Lord never ends!"

— LAMENTATIONS 3:22, NLT

These days, I embrace my forty years without God because it's like the Israelites wandering around the desert for forty years, attempting to get into the Promised Land. I was stumbling around in the backcountry, trying every which way to feel good—trying to get to my milk and honey land. My story could be a modern-day version of the Israelites' journey to Canaan. All of our stories are a journey of some sort, but it's the type of story we tell with our lives that matter. I want mine to be brilliant and beautiful, full of faith, hope, and love. Where are you in your journey to let Jesus love you?

NEVER FAILING ME

I like to journal my prayers to Jesus. I feel a strong connection with Him this way, and you might, too. Sometimes, He answers me with messages like the one I received while writing this chapter:

> *I am unfailing, I never let My children go. I hold on to all of them by their hands. I never let them go. They are Mine for all eternity and are all precious to Me. Everyone on earth can live in My love, refreshed and made whole. Your time has been marked with heart-break; this is true, but this is true for everyone. I tell you the truth, I will never let go of your hand.*

PRAY OR JOURNAL

You can pray for His unfailing love to pour out on you right now. Pick up your pen and your notebook, and in faith write out your thanks, your needs, your messes, and your failures. Ask Him to come help you. If you are writing and praying to Him from your lovely, soft, open heart, He will never fail to answer you. And remember, it doesn't have to be fancy. Simple is always good.

SOMETHING TO PONDER

Do you have a relationship with someone who never fails you? Do you have someone who is there for every mistake, blunder, or disaster you create, who never fails or leaves you regardless of them? What about the good things—the celebrations, job interviews, gallery openings, book signings, baby births—all the good news you want to share? Is there a person who is there for these too, never failing to love you exactly where you are at this exact moment?

> *"Let your unfailing love surround us, Lord, for our hope is in you alone."*

> — PSALM 33:22, NLT

THE CHASING GOD AND THE USED DAUGHTER

"What deep wounds ever closed without a scar?"
— Lord Byron —

"But the LORD God called to the man, "Where are you?"
— Genesis 3:9, NIV —

"Here I am! I stand at the door and knock."
— Revelation 3:30, NIV —

THE CHASE GAME

*W*hen I was a young girl, I was sexually molested by a man who was a friend to our family. Some friend. The stats show that 60 percent of sexual molestation[1] is perpetrated by a friend of the family. It's a high percentage especially since we entrust our kids to those friends.

It took place in the small house on the hill where I grew up. This older man made a game of it—the chase game. He would chase me into the bedroom where my brothers slept and would attack me there on the lower bunk bed. Then he would chase me again. If you ask me how long this went on or how many times he chased me, I couldn't tell you a definitive answer—I was six. What I do know is I can still feel this assault as if it happened yesterday. It's embedded. Please don't say to me it never happened, that I was too young to remember, or that I just imagined the whole thing. That's not an option.

I had the innocence to play the chase game and get caught. It was a game. I liked the game. It was male attention, and since I didn't have a father pouring out his love and affection upon me, the only attention available was through this friend of the family. For a love-starved six-year-old, any attention was better than no attention.

SALOME

Salome was another daughter who was used and abused for the secret purposes of others. Her story doesn't resolve the way I wish it would —with God swooping in to rescue her. In Scripture, she is referred to as a young, teenaged girl, and it reads like she was trying to please her overbearing, ambitious mother.

She isn't mentioned in many sermons I've heard, but she's the one who gets John the Baptist beheaded. She was a pawn in the marriage of her mom, Herodias, and stepfather, Herod Antipas, the ruler of Galilee, two famous and powerful people in those days. Salome ended up being used by them both to get what they wanted: Herod used her to impress influential men at his birthday banquet, and Herodias used her to get rid of the man who was causing her a lot of uncomfortable bad press. Who was that man? John the Baptist, Jesus' cousin.

Herod and Herodias divorced their spouses to marry each other, which is no big surprise to us in our modern world, except Herodias was married to Herod's brother, so they are already related to each other. John the Baptist had been putting their somewhat incestuous marriage into perspective for the people, proclaiming that what they were doing was immoral and prohibited in Jewish law during those ancient times.[2] This is the main reason Herodias wanted the prophet accusing her of an immoral marriage stopped. Herod wanted him stopped, too, so he threw John in jail to get him off the street, shutting him up until he could figure out what to do with him.

At Herod's birthday party, Salome danced to a room full of older men, and Herod, thrilled with her performance, says she can have anything she wants, promising, *"Whatever you ask I will give you, up to half my kingdom"* (Mark 6:23, NIV).

Salome ran to her mother for advice, and this was the perfect time for the mother to take control of the situation to get what she wanted. *"She went out and said to her mother, "What shall I ask for?" "The head of John the Baptist," she answered"* (Mark 6:24, NIV).

Salome went back to her stepdad and said she wanted the head of the prophet John on a platter. Herod knew where this request had come from, his jealous, entitled wife, but He couldn't lose face in front of these men who had just witnessed the dance and the promise. John was beheaded right then, and his head was put on a platter. Before she knew it, Salome was parading around the banquet with a platter and a head.

It's hard to believe she could have accepted the platter with his head on it, and that she walked around the room holding it until she finally delivered it to her mother. But she did. "I've done good, right?" might have been her question to Herodias, seeking approval, favour, and recognition. The story ends there with Salome placing the head in front of her mother at the banquet. Job well done.

There is an old saying from the nineteenth century that says the apple doesn't fall far from the tree, so perhaps Salome was like her mother after all and had as much of a part to play in the nasty beheading as Herodias did. I like to think she was a pawn because it's hard to believe a young girl could do this.

Jesus doesn't chase after Salome, or for any of them in the story. He certainly heard all about this event and immediately went off to a quiet place to grieve the death of his cousin, who was just murdered by a political leader. I wonder if he prayed for the young girl, Salome, used by others for their own evil purposes. Maybe He prayed for this girl to be saved; I hope so. Just as He chases after the one lost sheep, Salome would certainly be considered lost. History books say Herod and Herodias lost their power through war and ended up in exile, and Salome ended up freezing to death in a river on the way to join them.[3] None of their lives ended well because they never turned from their evil ways to God. There is always a better way.

We see in the story there was a pivotal point where Salome said yes when she could have said no. She could have made a better choice if she had the courage to face off against those who were using her. This is hard to do when you feel powerless. Was she so intent on pleasing everyone and getting their approval she didn't realize her own evil part in the murder?

THE SHAME OF BEING USED SEXUALLY

I know of another daughter who was sexually abused. I didn't know it at the time—I was too young to understand—but I know it now. She smelled funny and nobody liked her for this reason. She walked to school alone, holding her school books tightly to her chest, being teased along the way. She was always ill-kept, her hair greasy and flattened to her head, never shiny and blowing pretty in the wind. Her dress was always rumpled and dirty. I'll call her Tamar. I was in my thirties when I put two and two together and finally realized Tamar smelled of sex. Her father had been raping her.

In the schoolyard, shame was laid upon this poor girl's life and made her an outcast. This was terrible. I don't know if I joined in with the taunting of Tamar, but I observed it, afraid I'd be next in line. The boys were already teasing me for being an ugly "ostrich," and earlier, I'd been a victim to them shoving me into a pile of dog poop beneath a bush until a kind lady chased them off. Also, I had been molested, so I was a scaredy-cat, wanting to be invisible to the bullies.

I wish I had a happy ending to tell you about Tamar, but I don't. She endured a terrible childhood, and the kids in the schoolyard made it even worse by tormenting her. Oh, how my heart breaks for Tamar now as I write about her. Her story is the story of thousands of other young girls. Jesus' heart breaks every time this happens in our broken world, this sinful wrath upon the innocent. Why doesn't He stop it then, you ask? I'm still asking this question, and so are many scholarly, spiritual types worldwide. The answer isn't going to come from me because I don't know. He hasn't revealed this to me yet, except that I know He abhors sin, He works always for the good, and He has given us each a way to heal from our pain. I know He loves us unconditionally. He loves Tamar unconditionally and so deeply.

FORGIVING BRINGS FREEDOM

When I finally went to a counsellor after my first marriage disintegrated and before I became a follower of Jesus, the story of being molested and its effects finally caught up with me. I had never forgotten those events, but I had minimized them and stuffed them down. By doing so, I didn't believe they had an impact on my life, but I was wrong. The strategy during one of these sessions was to invite the molester into the room (figuratively), confront him, and then forgive him. Initially, this was terrifying; I didn't want him in the room, even if it was role-playing. I knew I had to work this issue out, so it took many sessions before I would allow him into the therapy room and for me to confront him—again through role-playing.

The counselling session helped me to let go of the fear of him, which was a positive measure, but in all honesty, I hadn't forgiven him quite yet. This was going to take something way bigger than myself.

Did I really have to forgive him? Jesus says we are to forgive not seven times but seventy-seven times—that is a lot of forgiveness. *I just have to forgive him the one time, right?* It was a lot to process for me.

Years later, after becoming a follower of Jesus, in prayer, I did forgive this man, but I don't want to give you the impression it was easy to forgive or that everything was la-dee-dah afterwards. There are many books, sermons, and papers written on the subject of forgiveness, and this isn't the focus of my book. I do want to suggest that forgiveness towards a person who has damaged you doesn't mean you agree with what they did, but it loosens their powerful, insidious grip upon your life. My experience was that the incidents faded away, which gave me freedom from them. I figure he is most likely dead by now, so there is no threat of him getting at me again. Besides, it is God's job to put him straight.

I've done enough thinking on this matter, writing in my journal and spending money on counselling sessions, but here I am again writing and crying about it one more time. It is for a different purpose now though. God has asked me to write about this experience because it's part of my story, which means it is part of His story.

These events contributed greatly to my "folding into myself"—inner withdrawal, tying knots in my heart, and carrying shame upon myself for many decades. This affected my world-view of men and, subsequently, my experience with them. I admit I have been afraid of men for much of my life, making it difficult to let one in. Or I did the complete opposite and let some loser in, and then, well, my life was a complete disaster. I believe my behaviour and poor relationship choices was a major result of being sexually molested by this older man.

Even now, I am curious what he must have said to me to keep me from telling my mom, but I will never know this. Did I believe, somehow, that because he was a familiar figure around our house, his actions towards me were part of the deal, part of the family? How did I come to believe this lie?

A FATHER'S CONTRIBUTION

Would having a father in my life prevented this sexual attack? Most likely. The missing pieces for daughters who don't have their dads around while growing up has a lot to do with how we value ourselves. A father's contribution is considerable in how we view ourselves, love ourselves, and navigate our life, especially with regard to the male population. From the book, *The Fatherless Daughter Project,* here are some of the things the authors suggest a girl receives from an available, good father.[4]

- Emotional, financial, and physical security;
- Forming boundaries on how to be treated and loved;
- Lessons in career, future aspirations, and financial management;
- When to speak up, take care, and hold strong;
- Positive model for an ideal husband;
- How to set physical and intimate boundaries with men;
- Self-worth developed by spending time together;
- Protection, knowing there is a warrior who will fight for them;
- Confidence and self-esteem developed through affection and words of encouragement;
- Perseverance to keep going and never give up, especially when things get difficult.

When I first became a follower of Christ, I have to admit I was miffed with God because I thought He was responsible for this happening to me. Where was He and why wasn't He in the room with me if He was supposed to be everywhere? Why didn't He stop it and how could He let a thing like that happen to a six-year-old girl? Many of you may also be wondering where God is in horrible situations and why He lets the suffering occur in the first place. This wasn't His plan at all. We live in a fallen world, and we have all turned away from God, every last one of us, doing our own thing until we feel good. Then, when it backfires, we do the next best thing to feel good again. When that doesn't work, we do another next best thing to feel good…until a six-year-old is being sexually molested on a bunk bed. I, too, for a good part of my life, have done this "next best thing" to feel good. I am a sinner, too. I am no better than the older man with his chase game. All of us have the nature of sin embedded in us, and we won't be getting rid of it entirely on this shore. God is broken-hearted over the consequences of sin in this fallen world and for this reason He has given Jesus to every one of us.

"For God so loved the world He gave His one and only Son, that whosoever shall believe in Him shall not perish but have eternal life."

— JOHN 3:16, NIV

He planned our hope and restoration before He formed the earth.

AN OPPOSITE PERSPECTIVE

"You hear, O LORD, the desire of the afflicted; you encourage them, and you listen to their cry, defending the fatherless and the oppressed, in order that man, who is on earth, may terrify no more."

— PSALM 10:17-18, NIV

Nowadays, I believe we simply aren't meant to know all the parts of the puzzle of our stories. Maybe if we knew everything, it wouldn't help us anyway, or perhaps we might further abandon God and never ask Him to help us ever again. Let me say this, God absolutely delights in helping His daughters, and He loves it when we ask Him to help us. Lately, I am asking God to help me see things in a different light and to help me understand what may have been going on for the other person involved (in any situation, not just this one). I now see if He had changed this part of my story, then my story wouldn't be my story anymore. I believe God did the most loving thing He could have ever done during those attacks—He prevented the actual rape, which would have been even more traumatic. This is what I choose to believe now, and for this alternative perspective, I am grateful because surely, I didn't come up with this idea on my own, Jesus did. He healed me through the forgiveness process, and my chains and memories were loosened. I am free. Now, I can joyfully declare: "God *was* in the room with me."

THE CHASING GOD

> "If a man has a hundred sheep and one of them gets lost, what will he do? Won't he leave the ninety-nine others in the wilderness and go to search for the one that is lost until he finds it? And when he has found it, he will joyfully carry it home on his shoulders."

> — LUKE 15:4-5, NLT

God will never stop searching for His kids—*never*—because He loves us. The promise in His Word is He leaves the ninety-nine and chases after the one who is lost. I was one of the lost ones. You might be a lost one too. He will not forget the one lost daughter out there walking towards the cliff about to stumble over to the rocks below. He won't do it. He will never, ever forget you. How do I know this? Because He saved me when I didn't even want saving. Heck, I wasn't even thinking about Him. In fact, I was doing everything I could to prevent God from finding me. He never gave up on me. His love chased me down, and He gave me my life back.

Slowly.

Masterfully.

He knew exactly how to woo me to Himself so I wouldn't do the same thing I did when the preacher chased me out of the church at the age of seven, terrified. He did this because He loves me no matter what a mess I am or how many mistakes I have made.

The Chasing God is the God who loves you so much that all He wants to do is move towards you with loving arms so you are not lost forever but instead, found. Maybe God is chasing after you right now —that's why you picked up this book and are reading it. He is showing you another way. Perhaps you are the one sheep who needs to know how much Jesus loves you. He is ready to take you into His arms and love you.

I want to encourage you to believe He adores you and values you so much. He made you as a blessing to our world. You are His beautiful daughter, and He wants you to be with Him in eternity. You hold a special place in His heart. He wants every one of us with Him. This is incredibly good news. Your mother may have given up on you, your father may have disowned you, or your spouse may have walked out and left you, but God never will. That's His promise to you, always.

> "Though she may forget, I will never forget you! See I have engraved you on the palms of my hands; your walls are ever before me."
>
> — ISAIAH 49:15B-16, NIV

Where is Tamar today? Did she become a social worker, an integral part of a counselling program for girls who have gone through the same thing she did? Or did she take her own life eventually? As I mentioned, I don't know what became of her, but I believe in God's plan for her, and so I have faith that He is always good and compassionate towards all he has made.[5]

Jesus would have pursued Tamar no matter how awful she smelled or how used and abused she was. He came to earth for all women—those who are sitting in fancy restaurants, looking so perfect in their Ralph Lauren suits as well as those who are sick, addicted, broken, and hurt. He pursues women walking towards the cliff, hoping to fall off the edge and fade away into darkness; women who think they are living a fabulous life but still have an emptiness in their soul; and women who are broken-hearted and barely coping, believing they have nowhere to go and no one to turn to.[6] He chases us all and never gives up. Ever.

FAITHFULLY CHASES US WITH LOVE

God never stops wanting His children to be brought under His protective wings. I want you to understand the urgency of Him moving toward you into your life and how important it is that you let Him love you. I mentioned before that God is a gentleman, so He is not chasing you to scare you or to send you running in the other direction. Instead, He pursues you with intentionality and persistence so as to love you. Over my lifetime, I can look backwards and see the times when God was in the room with me, urging me to come to Him and be His daughter, but I turned Him down. I had my own agenda to look after myself and do my own thing. The Marlboro woman, that was me. *I don't need anybody. I can do this on my own. I won't let anyone in to hurt me again.*

This way didn't work for me. I had no measuring stick except my own desire to feel better and to feel protected. I had nothing to guide, direct or show me a way. I created my own boundaries out of trying to protect my shattered heart. The Marlboro Woman approach works for the moment, but eventually that empty sadness returns. However, I discovered that when I said yes to Jesus and invited Him into my life, this deep, empty place inside of me went away.

That alone is enough to want Him. Then, oh then, *this* happened:

I wanted more of Him. I wanted to read His Word. I wanted to go to church every Sunday. I wanted to meditate on the words of God to find the hidden gems and gold nuggets. I wanted to meet and hang out with others who believe in Jesus, too. I wanted to give my money for His purposes. I wanted to go on a weekend retreat to dance, sing, and give Him praise all weekend long. I wanted to forgive the molester. I wanted to be forgiven for my part in shaming Tamar. I wanted to forgive my ex-husband for trash talking me and cheating on me. I wanted to write this book He has called me to write, even if it is uncomfortable to share the dark secrets of my soul.

All of these things I wanted to do because of Jesus. And I want more of Him still.

WRITTEN PRAYER

May I suggest a few things you can do?

Ask God for help. For a people-pleasing perfectionist with Marlboro Woman tendencies like myself, asking for help is probably the last thing you want to do. I get it…but do it anyways. He is waiting at the door for you to knock. He will come in.

Maybe written prayer works better for you, so grab your notebook, go to a park bench, the beach or a quiet corner in your home, and write it all out. Write with abandonment, knowing nobody else but God is going to read your words. Some of my closest encounters with God have been while I am writing my prayers to Him. Believe He is going to show up.

Have you read any Scripture yet? Consider borrowing or buying a Bible or downloading one on your smartphone and begin reading a few verses from it daily. The Psalms are delightful and poetic, while the books called John, Matthew, Mark, and Luke in the New Testament are bursting with God's love for you.

If you were sexually abused and have not talked to anybody about it, now could be a good time to consider this step. There are crisis centers and churches with effective programs and compassionate counsellors who can help you through the healing process. Jesus will heal your heart and help you to forgive those who hurt you as He did for me.

SOMETHING TO PONDER

Were you abused and used like Tamar and I were? Perhaps it was even worse for you. Have you kept your shame and pain hidden away all these years? Has it become unbearable, and you are wondering, *"Surely, there must be another way to live"*? Please consider Jesus. Say yes to His pursuit of you. If you have this book in your hand, He is pursuing you so He can love you. Your life matters to Him, and your eternal life depends upon giving your heart to Him.

My prayer for you:

LORD, protect your women, especially the precious one reading these words today. So many have been damaged and hurt by this world. Even their own families, especially their own families, were not the safe havens they needed for them to be. Our family is where we are supposed to be safe and protected, but to those who were shamed, abused, hit, ridiculed, or raped in the family, it was the least safe place for them. Lord, take away their pain and heal their broken hearts and souls. Replace all their pain with Your love. Oh, my Chasing God, show them the power of Your love in their life, and pursue them and bring them into Your arms. Move out towards each one of your daughters, and change their lives forever. Show them the power of Your steadfast love. In faith, I thank You that You hear my voice, and You hear the voice of these women who cry out to you. Amen.

THE WARRIOR GOD AND MARY'S SEVEN DEMONS

"The Lord himself will fight for you. Just stay calm."
— Exodus 14:4, NIV —

"Rise up, mighty God! Grab your weapons of war and block the way
of the wicked who come to fight me. Stand for me when they stand
against me! Speak over my soul: "I am your strong Savior!""
— Psalm 35:2-3, TPT —

JESUS IS BEAUTY

The only way I know to describe Jesus to you is to say He is the God of love, compassion, grace, mercy, kindness, reconciliation, and restoration. Could there be anything more beautiful than these things? These things may be at the heart of beauty. Can you think of love being anything other than the utmost beauty? Is compassion anything other than beautiful? And what of kindness, mercy and grace—are these anything other than the core of beauty? What about reconciliation with God? Now, that is utterly beautiful. Then there is restoration—Jesus came to bring the restoration of everything. Yes, the restoration of *everything*. You, me, nature—everything that is ugly, broken, and gone wrong with humanity and with our planet He came to restore it. Right now, today, He is restoring our hearts one by one. This is completely, supremely, and supernaturally beautiful.

Beauty comes alive in me because of Him, not because of anything I've done, and He will bring this same beautiful restoration for all who come to Him.

THE WAR ON WOMEN

"Every woman has a beauty to unveil. Every woman. Because she bears the image of God. She doesn't have to conjure it, go get it from a salon, have plastic surgery or breast implants. No, beauty is an essence that is given to every woman at her creation."[1]

— STASI AND JOHN ELDREDGE

There's a war going on, a battle for our souls. It's uncomfortable to discuss the adversary of our very souls, but I must because this warfare takes place every day. Right up front, I want to say I don't have all the answers (neither do many believers). What I do know is that this enemy is invisible to our natural eye which makes him incredibly sinister. Scripture tells us:

"For our struggle is not against flesh and blood, but against the rulers, against the authorities, against the powers of this dark world and against the spiritual forces of evil in the heavenly realms."

— EPHESIANS 6:12, NIV

So, I feel it's important to bring this fight to the light, knowing full well that with God everything is possible. Going one step further, I want to tell you about the battle I call "the war on women." I believe the enemy's most evil and hate-driven war campaign is against women. The enemy stands at the shore with his cold, lifeless eyes so livid that I even exist.

> *"Then the dragon was enraged at the woman and went off to make war against the rest of her offspring – those who obey God's commandments and hold to the testimony of Jesus. And the dragon stood on the shore of the sea."*
>
> — REVELATION 12:17: 13:1, NIV

I believe Satan hates women more than anything else. Why? Because we give birth to life, we carry the essence of beauty in us, and we have the feminine qualities of God deep within us, both relationally and spiritually. So if the devil can stop us from being God's beautiful daughters and from bringing life into the world, he can stop (so he thinks) God's love from expanding all over the world. John and Stasi Eldredge said it well in their book Captivating:

> "Put those two things together – that Eve incarnates the Beauty of God and she gives life to the world. Satan's bitter heart cannot bear it. He assaults her with a special hatred. History removes any doubt about this."

They went on further to say:

> "You are hated because of your beauty and power."[2]

Many people believe that Satan was once the most beautiful angel in Heaven.[3] Eventually his pride took over because of his beauty and then wanted all the glory and adoration for himself.[4] I have the notion the enemy is extremely jealous of women because we are more beautiful than he once was or will ever be again, so this is quite personal! If we believe in God, His kingdom, and all the miracles He does every day, we have to believe in all of it—including the devil and his part, not just the pieces we are comfortable with. We had better because the enemy is alive and well and fighting for our soul.

Most of us simply want to be at peace, safe, happy, free, in love, and enjoying an abundant life with a hope-filled future. Women, please listen, there is someone out there who doesn't want any of these things for you, and he most certainly doesn't want you to follow God and claim the beautiful life He has planned for you. Who do you think is the culprit who snapped shut the lock on your prison door?

The enemy is against women so vehemently he has chained some of us to a bed as a sex-slave worker, sold us at age eleven to an old man as a child-bride, mutilated us so we can't enjoy the sexual pleasure God designed for us, molested and raped us so we are shamed into silence and devaluation of ourselves, and (this is a really clever one) women's magazines all over the world tell us "you will never be good enough."

Yes, the enemy hates us and everything we represent, and he wants us to stop giving birth to more life and beauty. He wants us as far away from Jesus as he can get us. He's crafty and patient and clever. He is not in control of anything, by any means, but he is scrambling to devour anyone he can take with him before God throws him and his demons into the abyss forever.[5] Please don't let him take you.

I am writing as a way to connect with women who are feeling guilty for stopping a car in the crosswalk, who are living life with their shame glasses on, and who have hearts so tied up in knots there is nothing beautiful or enjoyable in their future. This is for women without hope, who are stuck because of the shame they carry with them from boardroom to boardroom, safe house to safe house, gym to gym, soccer field to soccer field, nightclub to nightclub, food shelter to food shelter, hospital room to hospital room. Please, please don't let the enemy take you.

I'd love for women's shame to be wiped away forever and for us to walk around freely in "who" we are. God created us in His own image and said we were good. Actually, God said we were very good:

"So God created human beings in his own image. In the image of God he created them; male and female he created them. Then God looked over all he had made, and he saw that it was very good!"

— GENESIS 1:27, 31, NLT

God's words in this passage clearly include women. Women, we are very good because He created us to be very good. And He loves everything He has created.[6] We need to soak in this truth, believe it for ourselves, meditate on it, and proclaim it for ourselves and our lives. This truth gave me hope that out of the ashes of shame, my beautiful, promised life could emerge. If you want to begin living a life of beauty —the abundant love God has for you—let yourself embrace this truth right away.

There is another truth I hope and pray you will grab onto just as quickly and firmly: God doesn't make mistakes. Therefore, you, by no means, are a mistake. You are exactly who God intended you to be. It has taken me decades to realize God's love for me, so I hope you will understand His truth sooner than I did. I gave up so much of my life wearing those harsh shame glasses and believing the lies.

My hope for you is that by knowing that there are other women who are stuck inside the prison walls of feeling shamed and unloved, you come to realize you are not alone, and there is another way to live. I hope that by reading this book a seed of light will be planted into your life.

MARY MAGDALENA AND HER SEVEN DEMONS

Was Mary accepted in her town? Did Mary fit in? Was she just not enough, or was she too much?

Mary had seven demons that she carried around inside of her. This was seven too many. Was she really possessed by seven demons or was she carrying around seven soul-sucking, negative mindsets? Was she ashamed, jealous, envious, hate-filled, self-absorbed, spiteful, or lustful? Maybe all of these. It doesn't matter because Jesus healed her from it all. If she had seven demons ruling her soul, then her life wasn't her own and everything she did was for evil intent and purposes. Everything she did would have been against loving herself, loving God, and loving others. She would have been filled with darkness, hate, and hopelessness.

Was she a prostitute? This is never mentioned in Holy Scripture about Mary. Not once. Could having seven demons ruling your life cause you to do some awful things? Absolutely. Perhaps prostitution was something Mary succumbed to, but I'm not going to agree too strongly with this one. There is evidence the persona of Mary being a prostitute was formed by Pope Gregory the Great,[7] of the early Western Christian Church, to detract from the love Jesus had for her and to diminish her importance to Him and His ministry on earth. I think this defaming of Mary has done the opposite—it has further cemented how much Jesus values women for our beautiful, female hearts and not for what we appear to be on the outside.

Thank you, Lord Jesus. You love us and do not condemn us for who we are or appear to be on the outside.

Whether she was a prostitute or not, it doesn't matter. Jesus healed Mary of her seven demons, obsessions, and pain points. If Mary was possessed by seven evil spirits, then Jesus performed the most amazing miracle on her, and likewise, if she was suffering from seven nasty "heart knots," Jesus performed the most amazing miracle there, too.

He turned her life upside-right and sideways. She became a new woman. As soon as Jesus spoke the words, she was released from the evil and hopelessness which had captured her soul; her burdens were lifted and became light. She could love again or maybe for the first time. And whose face did she see when the scales were peeled back from her previously darkened eyes? None other than Jesus Christ's. She immediately fell in love. From this point onward, she followed Him faithfully wherever He went.

All through the Judean countryside from town to town during his three-year ministry, she witnessed His divinity, power, and compassion for the downtrodden and ostracised, just like herself. She was dramatically healed and changed, going from seven demons (obsessions) ruling her life and then none! Freedom. To be healed from one obsession is enough to make me want to follow Jesus around for the rest of my life. What if He could heal your obsessions, addictions, and demons and show you another way to live, a life full of hope?

THE WARRIOR GOD

> *"Then I saw heaven opened, and suddenly a white horse appeared. The name of the one riding it was Faithful and True, and with pure righteousness he judges and rides to battle."*

> — REVELATION 19:11, TPT

Oh, Jesus, my Warrior God! He stands up and fights for women. One evening a few years ago, I had a strong vision of Jesus standing over me and a host of women, wielding a mighty sword up above our heads, guarding us with His supernatural shield, and proclaiming in His thunderous voice:

> *"You will not have my daughters. They are mine. My daughters will be with Me in My Father's house for all eternity. These precious daughters of Mine are off limits."*

I love this imagery of Jesus wielding a heavy sword above me while I sit at His feet, protected and safe. From this vision, I began to realise

Jesus fights for me. Shortly after this vision, verses from God's word seemed to pop off the pages into my heart, revealing to me how He fights and why I don't have to:

> *"For the battle is not yours, but God's. Do not be afraid; do not be discouraged. Go out to face them tomorrow, and the Lord will be with you."*

> — 2 CHRONICLES 20:15; 20:17B, NIV

There is a war taking place over us, but here's the good news: If you accept Him, Jesus wins every single time. Love always does. He fought for Mary and won. He fought for me and won. Imagine that, I'm saved into eternity.

HOW JESUS WINS

How did Jesus fight the battle and win? The Bible is God's love story of the redemption of planet earth and everyone in it. Your life has sin in it, whether you want to believe it or not, and just so you know, there isn't one person on earth who hasn't sinned. Not one.[8] So, you and I are not alone because we all carry around this propensity to sin within our soul. We seem to intuitively know this fact because we feel terribly guilty when we do or say something bad—well, most of us do—and we don't want to face up to the fact that one day we are going to have to pay for it.

God's price for all the wrong things we've done, to any degree, is blood; blood carries life in it, and blood cleanses. This is God's way. We are all going to be asked to pay for our wrongdoings one day with our life. This is where the beautiful grace of God comes in—He loves you so much He sent His son to be the blood payment for you. Instead of you "paying up" for your tarnished life, He has "taken the hit" by dying in your place.

Jesus is the Son of God, and He did it all for you by bleeding to death on a cross. He paid for all the little white lies, all the evil crimes you can imagine and everything in between for every person on earth—past, present, and future. Jesus arose on the third day, victorious over evil and death, so we don't ever have to go there ourselves.

That's right! God raised his dead body back to life. It's not a myth or an ancient tale. In fact, over five hundred of His followers actually saw Him alive after He died.

He wasn't a ghost or a spirit floating around the room—He walked and talked and ate breakfast with some of His disciples just like He had done before He died. One of His followers, Thomas, said he wasn't going to believe the truth of Jesus' resurrection unless he actually touched Jesus in the flesh and saw for himself. Later, he put his finger into Jesus' wounds and instantly believed Jesus was, indeed, the Son of God.[9]

Jesus' resurrection is another one of God's wonderful mysteries, and I like to think of it this way: God can do whatever He wants because He's the one with all the power. Plus, He promises us He will work out everything for the good. If Jesus were still dead and had never risen, He would be nothing more than another liar, making promises He couldn't keep, and our world would surely be a planet of darkness without any hope at all.

There is more to the story of how Jesus won. Forty days after His resurrection, Jesus returned to Heaven to be with His Father. He ascended into Heaven while some of His disciples watched this miraculous event. With His Ascension, Jesus completed the work of reconciling us all with Father God.

Jesus coming to earth, fighting the battle, and breaking death's grip on us is the "Good News." If you were the only person on earth, He would have still have fought, suffered, and died for you. He didn't hang on the cross for Himself; Jesus died there, dripping His blood for you, washing away the mess you've collected along the way walking out your journey. He fought for you there on the cross, and He will fight for you until you claim your daughterhood. This is The Good News.

TRULY A WARRIOR KING

There is no other power in the universe to match the power of Jesus, The Warrior God. Let this fill you with hope for a beautiful future.

I don't know about you, but I've had enough of my life taken from me. I've spent too much time with a negative disposition, trying to please others, living with a tormented mind, and never allowing peace and joy to enter. Joy was stolen from me, and sadly, I let it happen by not believing in God earlier in my life.

When I look back to who I was before knowing Jesus, I was this kid who wanted love so desperately but had no idea how in the world to get it. It was a tricky path to navigate, and I wasn't sure of the rules. Nobody set the rules out clearly or showed me where the good and safe path was. I had to discover this all on my own, where the good love was. It has taken me decades, and I don't want that for you. I want you to have hope and not waste any more of your one remarkable life by striving to find a better way.

You can be healed from your shame, pain, and insecurity and claim a beautiful life. What is holding you back? I hope the old adage, "better the devil you know than the devil you don't know," isn't a mindset holding you back because it's not a good idea to glob-on to that one. It's not better to know the devil. It's crucial you don't. His only tactic is to destroy lives and to keep everyone separated from God. He does this cleverly and brilliantly in the young hearts and minds of children, just like he did to me, and also in the hearts of adults. He will damage our lives if we let him. He will keep us miserable inside if we let him.

If anything keeps you dark, wretched, and away from the wonderful things of God (like love, peace, and joy[10]), it's from the enemy or from your own soul which leans, unfortunately, towards sin. Thank God, Jesus fought both of these and won. He doesn't want God's goodness to be absent from our lives. He wanted Mary free and living the good life He had planned for her. He definitely wants goodness for you, too, because you matter to Him and are a significant part of His divine plans.

I want a Warrior King. I want to be the princess to the Warrior King and allow Him to love me, guard me, take hold of my heart, strengthen my mind, and lead me into the life He has written for me. He has promised this for each one of us:

> *"Before I'd ever seen the light of day, the number of days you planned for me were already recorded in your book."*
>
> — PSALM 139:15-16, TPT

As it was in my case, the important thing to realize is you have to want to take the risk and allow Him to enter into your heart and life. If you do, He will fight for you right to the very end of time. Do you want a Warrior God? Jesus is The Warrior God, ready and willing to fight for you. You just have to stand under His sword, be still, and rest there, letting Jesus love you.

PRAY OR JOURNAL

May I suggest writing in your journal today, answering some questions. What are some of your "messed-up ways" that you want to change? What has kept you feeling small? Is it shame? Feeling unloved or insecure? What lies are you believing about yourself? Or are you just feeling sad and empty inside, sure that if you allowed the tears to flow, you would cry forever? That's how I used to feel—hopeless.

These are not easy questions, so you can always talk to God. Remember from previous chapters, praying doesn't have to be fancy —it's just talking. He's a great, big God, who can take it. After all, He made the universe and everything in it, so He can handle anything you throw at Him. I used to be so concerned about how I prayed—if I was doing it right and saying the right words. I wondered if I was praying too long or not long enough. Eventually, I gave up trying to follow anybody else's way, and now, I just say whatever comes out. Sometimes, I scream. Sometimes, I whisper. Sometimes, I write to Him. Sometimes, I apologize for being a jerk. Sometimes, I just say, "Help me Jesus," and this is usually enough.

SOMETHING TO PONDER

Ask yourself this: "Who fights for me?" Seriously, who stands over you, wielding the sword of truth and protection, proclaiming: *"You shall not have her. This woman has had enough. She is mine. She is my daughter, and she will be with Me in My House for all eternity. This daughter of Mine is off limits."*

As I come to the end of this chapter today, I hear Him whisper His promise: *"I will not leave them behind."*

THE PRISON-BUSTING GOD AND THE CROOKED WOMAN

"Some of us once sat in darkness, living in the dark shadows of death.
We were prisoners to our pain, chained to our regrets. For we rebelled
against God's word and rejected the wise counsel of God Most High.
So he humbled us through our circumstances, watching us as we
stumbled, with no one there to pick us back up.
Our own pain became our punishment.
Then we cried out, "Lord, help us! Rescue us!" And he did.

His light broke through the darkness and he led us out in freedom
from death's dark shadow and snapped every one of our chains. So lift
your hands and give thanks to God for his marvellous kindness and
for his miracles of mercy for those he loves! For he smashed through
heavy prison doors and shattered the steel bars
that held us back, just to set us free!"
— Psalm 107:10–16, TPT —

These verses show how deeply Jesus loves women—enough to bash through steel prison walls, grab scarred hands, and walk us out of our four walls of shame and pain. Nothing saddens God more than to have his daughters surrounded by prison walls. I hear Him saying: *"Tell my women I have come to break down the prison doors and bust them out."*

THE CROOKED WOMAN

She was a crooked woman, bound up for eighteen years, not straight but crooked. She was unable to look up into the sky above, to hold a toddler in her lap, or to look into her husband's loving eyes (if she had one).

Being hunched over for eighteen long, never-ending years, she must have been in pain every day. She was most likely sneered at, looked down upon socially, and pushed out of the way at the lineup for water at the communal well. Could she even lift the water pail into the well to draw water? She was likely teased relentlessly by children in the marketplace and men at the city gates, not to mention the women calling her nasty names within earshot. We all know how kind and sweet people can be, but we also know how incredibly cruel they can be, as well. This poor lady would be at the extreme end of being "different," and different can have unhappy consequences. Did she have a friend?

We know she was spiritually compromised because the thing that was causing her physical pain, discomfort, and shame was a spirit, and it was demonic. When I studied this story in the Gospel of Luke,[1] I found that each translation mentions the same cause: a disabling spirit (ESV), crippled by a spirit (NIV), crippled by an evil spirit (NLT), demonic spirit (TPT). She was in agony spiritually and mentally. Somehow, she had enough stamina and desire to get to the temple that morning, which, for the rest of her life, would be marked as the day she was set free. All she did was show up and move towards Jesus.

Jesus noticed her that day at the temple, bent over and crooked, enduring the pain and not complaining, and I believe He was touched. He hated the demon who bound her there. Perhaps, He said within

His heart, *This woman has had enough. I will change her life today. I will set her free. I won't put up with this for one more minute.*

Jesus had compassion for her and called her over to Him. Oh, to be called over by Jesus. He did the miraculous and placed His hands gently upon her, telling her she was free from her sickness.

How much do you think Jesus valued this woman? He broke the rule of the Holy Day to heal her body and fix her life; that's how much. It is interesting to me she didn't even ask for anything. She probably had reached a point of acceptance, thinking she would never be normal again. In fact, she likely believed this was her new normal, so she just had to find a way to cope. But God had a better plan for her life. She had endured enough already, and Jesus wanted her to have a better life, full of hope.

Right away she was healed. She stood up straight for the first time in eighteen years and looked into His eyes. What a set of eyes to look into after all those years! Can you imagine what it must have felt like to stand up straight after looking at your feet all this time? Can you imagine watching a bird fly again over the tops of trees in the bright blue sky, sleeping on your back, or hugging somebody after years of being bent over?

What happened next was so disappointing, though. While the "crooked-woman-made-straight" was dancing in the aisles and praising God, the leader of the temple didn't like Jesus healing on the Sabbath. He reminded everyone what the rules were: *"Six days you are to work,"* he shouted angrily to the crowd. *"Those are the days you should come here for healing, but not on the seventh day!"* (Luke 13:14, TPT).

He might as well have said, "We don't want to see God working any miracles today." This poor woman was experiencing the best day of her life, standing tall and praising God, and she got shamed and embarrassed once again.

Jesus must have been steaming with indignation by then, so I love what He did next. He didn't put up with any nonsense and told everyone at the synagogue how valuable and precious this woman was to God. Hallelujah! Jesus stood up for this woman and declared that, after what she had gone through all those years, she shouldn't have to wait one more minute to be set free. These are His exact words:

> "You hopeless frauds! Don't you care for your animals on the Sabbath day, untying your ox or donkey from the stall and leading it away to water? If you do this for your animals, what's wrong with allowing this beloved daughter of Abraham, who has been bound by satan for eighteen long years, to be untied and set free on a Sabbath day?"

— LUKE 13:15-16, TPT

Jesus set her free immediately.

THE PRISON OF SHAME

Shame holds women in prison. Shame keeps our lives small. Shame says we are never good enough, never enough. And shame also says we are just too much—too much to handle. Well, what is it then— never enough or too much? Shame is every lie you ever heard about yourself that tied your heart up in knots and kept you small. Could shame be what has kept you from claiming and living the beautiful life God has designed for you?

For me, I felt like I was never good enough. Who told me this lie? I know who the enemy is, but who did he use to get to me? Who has he used to get to you? Shame does an excellent job at keeping us feeling insignificant, and girlhood shame seems to run quite deep.

For the soft-hearted, highly sensitive types like myself, I wasn't brave enough at six years old to reject and cast down the bitter lies I heard. Instead, I absorbed them deeply, became them, lived them. A heart under attack becomes hardened in the protecting process, knot by knot. A solid mass of knots becomes steel around our tender, pliable hearts. It's a prison. How do we ever get out of this prison?

What has helped me so far is knowing and believing I have value in God's eyes. This is an upside-down perspective because culture and history teach us that women are really not too important, irrelevant, not to be taken seriously. Let me tell you what Jesus teaches by His words and actions. Get ready to love yourself the way God does and walk right through those prison doors because Jesus' encounters with women while He walked to earth are encouraging and full of loving-kindness, mercy, and grace.

WHERE THE LIES COME FROM

It was summertime, and I adored my two friends who lived down the hill—two sisters with long, blond hair sweeping up into ponytails and revealing their pretty blue eyes. They were so different than me. I always had the boyish, pixie haircut and boring, brown eyes. Back in those days, women visited women. They walked to each other's homes for a cup of coffee after the housework was done. Nobody phoned anybody; they just showed up, and the hostess was always prepared with some delicious, homemade cake and a pot of tea or coffee.

My two blond friends and their mother walked up the hill one day for such an occasion as this—to drink some tea, have a slice of cake, and (no doubt) gossip about the neighbours. We girls got bored soon enough hanging out with our mothers, and we headed out into the yard. We lived in the middle of a steep hill, so our back porch was on stilts, and we could actually play under the porch.

As young girls did at our age, we were discovering our bodies. And guess what we were having a look at? Yes, that spot. "What's that?" "What does it do?" "Yours looks funny." "So does yours." We hadn't noticed the younger sister had slipped away while we were having a look. Before the two of us knew what was happening, my mom showed up with a broom handle in her hand, screaming and cursing at me.

"You filthy little girl!"

I ran. She chased me around the yard and beat me with the broom handle—not just once. I ran again. She beat me again. After a beating, who is ever the same again? I wasn't. The shame of it all was devastating. To be beaten in front of my two friends was beyond humiliating. I was beaten for being curious. What did this say about my body? *Your body is a horrible thing. You should be ashamed of yourself. You should know better.*

If it wasn't enough for the grown-ups to cover us with shame, the school yard also provided ample opportunity for it to be smeared upon our souls. I was tall and gangly with long, skinny legs and arms. Nothing fit me correctly; pant legs and sleeves were always too short. All the other kids had pants long enough to drape perfectly over their shoes, but not me. No matter how much I pulled to stretch my pant legs longer so I could fit in, they didn't, so I didn't.

The kids in the school yard were brutal back then, so anyone "different" was a target. I was a target for being a tall, gangly girl. The boys in my class called me "Ostrich." They taunted me with this nickname relentlessly. I was ashamed I had such an unappealing body, and I believed nobody liked me because of it. I was ashamed my clothes didn't fit and my legs were too long.

"Ostrich," I adore the name now because I've seen ostriches up close in the wilds of Africa, and they are rather interesting birds, indeed. Yes, gangly. Yes, tall with skinny legs, but their sweet, comical faces and swiftness in running I find quite attractive.

I wish I could pick up my little-girl-self in the schoolyard, hold her in my arms, and explain to her how cool and grand an ostrich really is, to empower her with hope, goodness, love, and value instead of the shame. Oh, I think I just did.

What happened then when I put on a bathing suit? Of course, it didn't fit. Do they ever? Spending a few weeks every summer on my grandmother's farm was a rich experience I treasure because of her loving sweetness and also for the food she made, for time with my cousins, and for the wonderful lake. One of my aunts would pile us all into her car along with beach blankets, a basket of food, and drinks and take us all to the beach to swim each afternoon. On one of those afternoons, I was crushed to hear a group of teenage boys and girls (the cool ones) pointing at me and saying with snickers, "Wow, look at the long one!" I was the long one, the one who didn't fit in with their cute, bikini-perfect, teenage bodies. I was different, and they sure let me know it with their cutting words. Again, I felt ashamed of my body.

My glamourous aunt witnessed the pain and embarrassment I had received, and she offered me kind words out of earshot of the cool kids: "There will come a time in your life when you will love your long legs." She was right. A smile and a few words of building up instead of tearing down were powerfully kind acts for my tender heart. If we would only practice this daily, we would change our world.

YOU ARE TOO SKINNY

There was a young woman in our town (still living with her parents), who once a week, would come out to our farmhouse after dinner for a cup of coffee. She seemed lonely to me because she was quite a bit younger than Mom, and I knew she wasn't coming out to visit me. She did most of the talking and was hard to get rid of once she had her foot in the door—muffled yawns didn't work. One night, she came to visit and as the hours were wearing on and enough yawns were muffled to sink a battleship, Mom finally slipped off to bed, leaving me alone with her. She gossiped about the teachers at the school, probably the only thing we had in common, then she said it: "You'll never get a boyfriend. You're too skinny. Men like women with a bit of meat on their bones, and you don't have any, so you'll never get a boyfriend looking the way you do."

Gee, thanks, that's exactly what an insecure teenage girl like me needs to hear. How am I ever going to get a boyfriend looking like this? And being flat-chested to boot made me feel even more unwanted by the male population. So where did I go from there except to continue believing the lies—more lies that nobody loved me or would be loving me any time soon, especially, looking the way I did. *Tie a knot.*

These are the types of lies the enemy uses to devour our life, keeping us small and tormenting us throughout our lifetime. Words sting and shape. Sad to say, we humans haven't figured out yet that our words matter—good or bad. Words matter because today, six decades later, I can still feel the sting of those cruel words dragging me backwards to a gangly, skinny, teenaged girl who didn't fit in.

RIGHT HERE AND RIGHT NOW

Here's the good news though: Jesus loves me right here and right now. I don't have to get organized and cleaned up, wear long enough pants, look good in a bathing suit, or be "in" with all right spiritual people, and then maybe He will love me. That's like cleaning the house before the housecleaner arrives.

Perhaps some of you believe you only deserve love once certain conditions are met—if you look pretty, have a perfect body, talk intelligently, make a pile of money, drive a bigger car, own a mansion, and on and on—then they will love you. That's exactly how I used to think. *What do I have to do to get loved?* That was the huge, unanswerable question in my heart for so long.

Many relate God's love to how they experienced the love from their earthly fathers as kids. What happens when there is no earthly father on the scene or when he's an abusive father and doesn't treat his children well? Some who were treated with physical abuse might think God is cruel and mean. A girl who was driven by her dad to the point of perfectionism because nothing was ever good enough for him, might view God as a task-master with never-ending good works required in order to get acceptance and love. For some of us with no experience of a father because he was absent, the connection of what God might be like is so vague there is nothing to grasp onto or understood. For me, the concept of God was missing—just like my dad.

But God didn't abandon me. Even when I was wandering around in the wilderness all those years, pacing about in my own self-made prison of bad choices and searching for love in all the wrong places, He never let go of me. When I finally got tired of the mess I was living in, God provided me with a way out—Jesus.

THE PRISON-BUSTING GOD

Every woman is God's special creation whom he loves and adores. He will do anything and everything He can to take us out of our self-made prison cells into His gracious light, where following Him is easy and light.[2] He hung on a cross two thousand years ago to show you how much He cares for you, and as I've said before, if you were the only woman on earth, He would still have died on the cross so you could be set free from your prison.

> "Lift up your heads, O you gates; be lifted up, you ancient doors, that the King of glory may come in. Who is this King of glory? The Lord strong and mighty, the Lord mighty in battle. Lift up your heads, O you gates; lift them up, you ancient doors, that the King of glory may come in. Who is he, this King of glory? The Lord Almighty – he is the King of glory."
>
> — PSALM 24:7-10, NIV

Gates and ancient doors—what do they mean? Maybe in ancient times, they symbolized a fortified, walled city, where through the gates and doors, the saving king could enter and save the city. Perhaps to lift up the heads of gates and doors is telling us to stop sleeping, stop slumbering, and stop being unaware. There is another way to live. Something better is approaching. Something more. Something worth lifting our rusted-out mind and heavy-burdened heart for. The King is coming to save us.

What are the fortified walls protecting? Your heart? That wall was built up over time through the sorrows of childhood abuse, words ripping through the heart, a cuff across the face, or a swat for saying innocent words they didn't want to hear. The wall was built to comfort us so we could escape behind it.

Oh, these gates, these doors... Are these the openings to our heart? Even an old, ancient, rusted heart has an opening somewhere. If we would lift up our heads and look upwards, out of ourselves, towards Jesus, then the fortified walls can be penetrated through the rusted gate and heavily tarnished door. It's there, the opening to our closed-off heart. We invite the Prison-Busting God in by lifting up our heads. We make the first move because He is already and always right there ready to push open the rusted gate and tarnished door. The King of Glory waits for us to lift our heads, the heavy gateway into our hearts; look to Him, and invite Him in.

TRULY BUSTS US OUT

When we are sick to death of our fortified walls—all those bricks, stones, and mortar that have kept our hearts and souls captured inside —He will come in mysteriously and powerfully, bringing His hope and glory into the dark corners of our empty, sad spirit. The King of Glory. He is here.

This Prison-Busting God is available to everyone, including you, but only if you really want Him. Jesus set the crooked woman free from her prison of a broken body and spirit, and she became filled with His love, goodness, and peace. Right now, wherever you are at this moment, Jesus will grab your hand, pull you up, and set you on the path to freedom simply by you asking for His help. It means believing in Him as the One who can set you free and then trusting He will do it.

PRAY

Thank you, Jesus, You fight for me and win. Thank You, Jesus, You love me so much You are willing to drag me out of my prison of lies and out of the small life I am living. Thank You, Jesus, You will shine Your light continually and endlessly in my heart. Even when I mess up tomorrow and the next day, You will come back for me and fight again and again, and You will never let me go. I don't know where you are taking me, and I don't care as long as I am going with You. Your true light is all I will ever need. Amen.

SOMETHING TO PONDER

Do you want to change by giving up the thing you've been living in captivity with, such as alcohol, adultery, drugs, stealing from your employer, anger, jealousy, excessive spending or eating, on and on? Think about it, and be honest with yourself; do you really want to give it all up? Then, once you walk out of your prison doors, are you willing to stay out? Jesus can help you with this, too. It means letting Jesus love you.

"The true light that gives light to everyone was coming into the world."

— JOHN 1:9, NIV

THE INVISIBLE GOD AND THE
WIDOW WITH TWO COINS

"For since the creation of the world God's invisible qualities—his eternal power and divine nature—have been clearly seen, being understood from what has been made, so that people are without excuse."
— Romans 1:20, NIV —

"All honor and glory to God forever and ever! He is the eternal King, the unseen one who never dies; he alone is God. Amen."
— 1 Timothy 1:17, NLT —

I believe in The Invisible God. You might want to consider this, too. It could explain some things in your life as it helped to reveal some things in mine.

Think of a time when you got into a car late at night with somebody you shouldn't have, drank yourself silly, and then walked down a dark alley at 3 a.m. Then you let someone shove another hit of LSD into your mouth, were given the date-rape drug, and woke up in a police station six hours later. Or what about the time you were waiting for the school bus and an older man pulled up beside you asking if you wanted a ride, saying your parents had sent him to pick you up? Some of these things have happened to me, some of them to people I know. Can you think of a time like this for yourself? Should we credit it to chance that, luckily, it turned out okay in the end? Are we saying: "Boy, you were lucky that time—it could have been so much worse." And if it didn't turn out okay, are we then the first to blame God? Where was God in all this? I am suggesting it is The Invisible God in the corners of the room with us. Who do you think orchestrated the police officer to check out the girl slumped over in the back alley, unconscious, clothes torn off? How can we explain the evil kept at bay while we walked down the alley-way drunk, staggering to get home? What made your senses tell you to run the other way as fast as you could when that pedophile asked if you wanted a ride home? And how could our fragile body handle another dose of drugs shoved into our mouth at the party? Could it have been the Invisible God's protective hand? I know of only one person who would do all of these things for me—The Invisible God.

I want to tell of a few times when The Invisible God showed up in my life. I revisit these scenes over and over, and for some reason, although small events, I have never forgotten them. I believe God was there, even though I didn't believe in Him at the time—more than that, I didn't even want Him in my life. The stories are important to share, not only because He asked them to be shared but because they give glory to The Invisible God. I believe He appoints angels to look after us. Oh, thank You, Jesus, that You are alive and everywhere, even though I can't see You.

He whispers into my heart while writing this book: *My protective angels were in the corners of the room; we were watching over you. Our power was there. For all the boys and girls who were hurt, shamed, and bullied, I was there to protect them. I was in the schoolyard. I was in the cloakroom when the door was shut, and you were being attacked by boys. I did stop them from going further and further. I did this through people, teachers, caregivers, parents, sisters, brothers, and grandparents.*

HE WATCHES

One summer, I went away to a resort town with a girlfriend to get a job and make some money. This was a tourist town up in the mountains. Kids like us came from all across Canada to work the summer months and make a bit of money. There were many of us teenaged workers looking for a place to stay, so we ended up homeless on the streets for the summer. I was sixteen.

We worked in several places and slept in several places: in parks, in washrooms in the parks, under the overhang of the entrance way to an elementary school, down by the river, and in our sleeping bags under a bush. Occasionally we were able to stay in somebody's room, whom we'd met that day, which was great except we'd be back out on the street the next morning. We met many boys and quickly fell into the bar scene. It was easy to get in underage; the beer was cheap, and it was somewhere to go until closing time and we had to find a place to sleep again.

One night my girlfriend and I were separated for some reason, and I was left alone at the beer parlour to find a place to stay. A big, handsome guy with long, flowing, hippy hair, who I'd seen in the bar a few nights previously, offered me the back of his truck to sleep in if I wanted it. This seemed like a reasonable thing, and fueled by beer, I agreed.

He drove us to the outskirts of town into the dark night, and while I was a bit concerned by his departure from town, I went along with it. He was a good-looking guy, and we had an attraction for each other, but I was still surprised to find that the back of the truck included him being there, too. This is when I got a bit nervous; I was alone in this truck with a big, muscular guy in the isolated outskirts of town. What had I just done? He proceeded to become physical with me, and it was obvious he wanted sex. How naïve could I possibly be?

I said no. He became a bit more aggressive, and I said no again. Soon he was on top of me, and as I mentioned, he was big, outweighing me by probably seventy-five pounds. I said no again and then told him I had only come out here to sleep in the truck, like he had offered. I didn't want to have sex. Did I cry? I may have.

Suddenly, he stopped his aggressive sexual moves, and I asked him to sleep in the cab of the truck. He didn't have to listen to me—it was his truck, and he could have overpowered me in a second. He finally agreed. This is the closest I have come to being raped as a teenager.

I believe to this day the angels assigned to me were working that night. I was in a dangerous position, yet because of the work of my assigned angels and God looking out for me, I was spared being raped. I have confidence this was God's protection over me because this incident remains with me. It went well for me when it could have been disastrous. I believe God wants me to remember it and to know, without a doubt, He protects those He loves. He also wants me to pass this truth on to others by sharing my story.

LEAVING HOME FOR THE CITY

When I left home, I had a few bucks in my pocket, a bus ticket in my hand, a certificate announcing I was a secretary, and a piece of paper with an address. I had sewn a few outfits for the move to the city, and those were packed away in a battered, orange suitcase. I was heading to a city I had never been to before—heck, I hadn't even *been* to a city. I was sure my life would be taking on glamourous portions, and dreams of satin gowns and cigarette holders danced in my mind. I would impress everyone back in my hometown with my independence and courage... *Boy, I'll sure show them.* I was seventeen and fresh off the farm.

My mom had arranged a place for me to stay for a few days—the piece of paper gave the name "Liz" and her address. All I had to do was get off the bus at the Greyhound station and catch a cab to the address shown on the paper. Liz was working late, so she said she would hide a key under a flowerpot and for me to go on inside. I was to take the bed in the back bedroom, and we would sort the rest out in the morning. Seemed simple. Except it was pitch dark, and I couldn't find the house on either side of the street. Now what?

I trudged up and down the street one more time, lugging my suitcase, looking for the house. Nothing. I was close to tears and sick of lugging my purse and suitcase when I heard a voice in the dark: "Can I help you? You seem lost." I swung around and there was a man standing there. I was startled and fear began to creep in.

"Well, I'm looking for the house I'm staying at, and I can't find it. Do you know where 1028 is?"

"Okay, so let's see." And he walked up the street a few houses and then back along the other side. "There is no 1028. Are you sure you have the right address?"

I looked at the piece of paper. "It says 1028."

"Let me see." I handed him the paper. "Oh, you're looking for 1028 East 11th—this is East 10th. That's just around the corner."

"But I've never been to the city before, so I don't even know how to get there. The cab was supposed to drop me off out front."

"Don't worry, hop in my car, and I'll drive you there," he said. And he did. Five minutes later, I was in Liz's apartment with the door locked safe inside.

This was The Invisible God. His protective hand upon my life once again and I didn't even know it.

ENCOUNTERING THE INVISIBLE GOD

"For he will order his angels to protect you wherever you go. They will hold you up with their hands so you won't even hurt your foot on a stone."

— PSALM 91:11-12, NLT

I mentioned the little house on the hill where I lived with my mom and siblings before she remarried, and we moved out to the farm. It was all my single mom could afford at the time. It had a living room, a kitchen, two bedrooms, a bathroom, and a short hallway connecting up the rooms. Today, we still marvel how she managed to pull off getting a mortgage and buying this little house without a husband, but she did.

When I was nine, I was left home alone on many Friday nights while mom took my two younger brothers into town grocery shopping, a payday ritual for many families. My older brother and sister were with their friends having fun. I stayed in the kitchen, huddled on a chair at the old, worn-out kitchen table, clinging to the kitchen wall, which I figured was somehow friendlier than being out in the open and exposed. (Exposed to what? I wasn't sure, but I was terrified of it.)

I sat and read my book, waiting for mom to come home. My eyes often wondered off the page to search the kitchen for something scary, perhaps the glowing face of an old man gawking in the window, a ghost, or a crazy old woman. There was no end to the scary possibilities my imaginative, young mind could conjure up of frightening creatures creeping about the house while the hot hiss of coal burning in the furnace and the sound of the tree branches clawing against the kitchen window spooked me even further.

Oh, when will they get home? Just come home quick, please! Where are you, mom? Why was I left alone again?

I was near tears, and my senses were heightened; every bark from the neighborhood dogs sent my stomach jumping into my throat. My eyes darted every which way in search of something not of this world, something dark and evil.

Suddenly I felt the hair on my arms stand up as though something really was in the house with me now. I moved only my eyes and looked towards the living room and saw nothing; I looked back to my book and clung closer to the table. I watched. I waited. I wasn't reading anymore, but I didn't move so the evil thing would think I was reading and leave me alone.

My senses were electrified as I sat scared and alone, when I felt two hands gently touch my shoulders and stay there for a few minutes. I didn't move a muscle or blink. I didn't scream or cry or vomit even though I wanted to do all these things at once. I stayed motionless until I felt the hands move away, taking their warmth with them. After the hands left my shoulders, I remained there, still. *Am I still breathing?*

Then something wonderful happened. I felt the terror rise out of me and float away, and in its place, I felt warmth and calmness. Fear replaced with courage, I got up and walked around the kitchen and into the bedrooms. I felt safe. I wasn't afraid anymore. I wondered what had just happened. A few minutes later I heard the car engine from mom's old, green station wagon as it chugged up the hill and pulled into our driveway.

Whose hands were laid upon my skinny shoulders to calm and comfort me that night? Was it Jesus? Was this one of God's angels? Do I believe there are heavenly angels assigned to look after children when they are so terrified and alone they need comfort? Do I believe God was with me that Friday night? I do because I know somebody touched me that ominous night. I can still feel His hands upon my shoulders and the experience of the fear floating away.

This was The Invisible God. His protective hand was displayed upon my life once again, and I didn't even know it.

FAILED MARRIAGE

The introduction to this book ended with a failed marriage, in a bleak basement full of dark, dusty windows and spiders. I can still feel the desolation as I write about it now. The musty, crowded, cement walls lined with boxes full of junk made it seem like a place of bottomlessness, something to climb out of. Still, I didn't meet God there. I did not cry out to Him. I didn't know Him. I didn't *want* to know Him. He wasn't even on my radar and certainly was not a desire. He was as absent (so I thought) as my earthly dad was.

I had a precious friend once, Kathleen, who simply asked: "How are you doing?" I was ten years into an unhealthy, destructive marriage.

"Oh, just fine."

Isn't this a typical reply we all use whether in crisis or in delight? "Yup, good, I'm fine. Doin' great." Who wants to reveal the ugliness of their own reality to anyone? Not me. I couldn't handle the intimacy... *I don't know how it works, and by the way, it's too risky anyway.*

Intimacy was frightening to me. It still can be at times, but I know it is the only way to love, and besides, I'm working on it. This is what I believed back then: *If I start to cry, I will open up and cry forever; my tears will never stop. I will cry a river right straight through to the wide-open ocean. The wounds are too wide, like a never-ending sea of pain, loss, and rejection. This is why I can't tell the truth to her when she asks me—especially in a coffee shop sharing a muffin together. I will cry a river.*

"No. I mean *really.* How are you doing?" The second time around she was asking for the truth.

It made a crack in the stone—it was the question which cracked my heart of stone. You see, I'd been wearing a mask of stone to show the world how tough I was, how independent and resilient I was. It hid my truth—the lies I believed that nobody really loved me anyway... *I know exactly how to hide this pain every day. How can I live in a world that is short on love, full of rejection and darkness? Well, I will build a mask of stone and a heart of steel knots—nobody needs to know me. This is what I do and what I have become. Since nobody loves me, then, I mustn't love me either. But I look pretty. Maybe somebody will love me just for that...* And most of them did.

"Not here." My face cracked. A sliver of hope entered my heart, just a glimmer. I didn't need to tell her the mess I was in because she could see the sadness and despair painted all over my face.

"I have no place to go."

"You can stay with me." And so began a chapter of both darkness and light. This is how I ended going from husband, dog, house, china plates, coffee tables, plants, dish towels—my whole life—all left behind to a basement of cement and cobwebs.

Sickness, darkness, and the deepest despair I could fall into was in this basement full of boxes with no light. Days of laying on a pullout couch, drinking lemon and water, losing pounds, and breathing ragged breath. No light. Nothing to hope for and nothing good to grasp. *Can it get any worse than this? Perhaps crack houses are like this— they probably are.* It was my dear friend's basement and she offered it up so sweetly to help me get free from a marriage so wrong and dangerous. *If I had stayed in that destructive marriage any longer, I would be gone. Never mind, I already am...*

Soon after I moved into her basement, my nightmares subsided, and I wasn't afraid to fall asleep anymore in fear of another horrific dream of clawing monsters.

Kathleen was there and her friend Jenny. I climbed the stairs up out of the dark basement one day, and they were there, the two of them, laughing, sipping coffee. They were normal. Why did I even ask about the Bible on that particular day? I don't know because I wasn't really interested.

"Oh, ask Jenny about the Bible—she's the one who knows it so well. I just go to church and know a little bit about it," she said.

She told us she actually got saved in church and was now born-again. *Born what?* I remembered how her boyfriend used to roll his eyes at the new friends she was hanging out with—these insane, born-again Christians.

She told me her brother died in a climbing accident, and she was broken to pieces over losing him. She said she became a believer because she wanted to see her brother again, and she knew she would see him in heaven one day because he was a believer, too. But she didn't know the Bible that well, not like Jenny—Jenny knew the Bible. She grew up a missionary's kid.

Jenny shook her head and chuckled. "Oh, the weirdos who showed up at our house—we weren't normal. Every night there was somebody different at our kitchen table. There were always strange people around our house. We weren't a normal family." She seemed a bit miffed just by talking about it, so I didn't bother to ask her anything more about the Bible.

It was Kathleen who planted the seed that day. Kathleen told me she was the only one in her family who was a follower of Jesus. "I have nothing to lose by believing in Jesus." And in that, I now know, she meant she had everything to gain.

I call Kathleen "my angel friend" because she gave me a place to go when I'd hit rock bottom. My life was bleak and hopeless, and then she planted a seed. Still, I didn't believe in God, but The Invisible God knew what He was doing all along. He had it all worked out. He knew exactly what I was going through and who to put in my path—this was no surprise to Him. Now I can look back and see what I couldn't see then.

Oh, Lord, for Kathleen, I will always be eternally grateful.

I eventually lost touch with Kathleen, seeing her only a few more times before she moved away to Toronto. Then she seemed to disappear. We've all heard the saying: Friends come into our life for a reason, a season, or for a lifetime. Was she there only to get me further down the road toward the Lord and give me a true-life pain and sorrow example as to why I need Jesus so much in my life?

A pilgrimage had begun, except I didn't know it at the time. The path to salvation, forgiveness, thanksgiving, rightness, reconciliation, healing, goodness, and beauty was opening up for me. I didn't know this then, only God knew the path I was on. She planted the seed, and today, I can't be without Him.

This is why it is so fabulous I get to wear the princess crown today—the crown which declares I am His daughter and He loves me. Actually, it is a small ruby ring on my right-hand ring finger which reminds me every day of His love. This little ring says I now have a father who tucks me under His wings like a hen with her baby chicks. He stands over me and fights, declaring His love to me through blessings and grace cascading into my life. Oh, but it wasn't always this way.

THE WIDOW WITH TWO SMALL COINS

She walked into the temple one day and dropped two small, copper coins into the offering box. She was a poor woman and her resources were limited. She wouldn't be earning an income anytime soon, and she had no husband to replenish the cash box with a paycheck—he was long gone and so was the income he provided.

The poor widow had one option: to believe in The Invisible God to provide food and shelter to her for the rest of her days. *God will see what I have given and will provide for me* were her thoughts as she dropped the coins in. It was all she had left, but she wanted to give them anyway. She had a deep faith in God even if she couldn't see Him there in the temple. *I know my precious God is here somewhere.*

With the sound of the coins hitting the bottom of the box, she got noticed. Jesus saw her drop the coins in, and surely, His heart must have leapt with love and joy for her. He pointed her out to the men who were following him and said:

> *"I tell you the truth, this poor widow has given a larger offering than any of the wealthy. For the rich only gave out of their surplus, but she sacrificed out of her poverty and gave to God all that she had to live on, which was everything she had."*

— MARK 12:43-44, TPT

The widow had a deep faith in God and practiced the truth of sowing and reaping. Whatever we sow, we reap. She believed in something way more powerful than that though—she believed God was the source of everything. He was her source for money, food, shelter, shoes, clothing, and so on. Even though she could not see this unseen God, she gave Him everything she had because she knew this was the only way to live. She had given her heart to God. She had said yes.

I can only imagine that she had been living this way since her husband died, leaving her with barely enough food to eat. She had never been forgotten or abandoned, and she had never gone hungry. She always had bread, olive oil, water, and a table to serve it on. She always had a coin to put into the offering basket even if it was the last coin in her skirt pocket and even if she never knew how it mysteriously got there —she had it to give.

Jesus did not let this small scene go unnoticed and instead uses her actions and her story to show His followers how to live in complete reliance upon an unseen and Invisible God. She was a little old lady with a tiny story to tell, but Jesus loved her so much He gave her a place of honour among the men in the temple. *See how much she loves God, how deep her faith is—you should be doing the same.* Actually, He honoured her with a place in eternity! Here we are, women in the twenty-first century, reading about her today and admiring her faith, in awe of the love she had for God. Jesus brings glory to God through this woman.

THE INVISIBLE GOD

"He is the divine portrait, the true likeness of the invisible God, and the firstborn heir of all creation."

— COLOSSIANS 1:15, TPT

God is unseen but He is with us in many ways revealing Himself to us. Have you ever walked through the rainforest and thought to yourself, "I can smell God"? Have you ever sat at the seashore, listening to the waves as they calmed your frazzled nerves? Have you ever spent hours climbing a mountain and heard a small voice welcoming you when you reached the top? Have you ever gazed into the intricate details of a flower blossom and felt your heart about to explode for the simple beauty of it? Have you ever plucked a wild blackberry off a bush in an alpine meadow mid-summer, popped it in your mouth, and thought, "Oh, this is heaven"? I have.

These are all reminders of God. Since we can't see Him with our natural eye, He has given us other ways to see Him. I can't deny God is all around me when these wonders of the natural world He has created appear everywhere I go. I was surprised to smell God in the rainforest that day and began to laugh. How did He know where I was? There was no doubt I was smelling the aroma of God in the forest. Oh my.

THE AMAZING INVISIBLE THREE

We've all heard it said, "God is good"[1] and "God is love."[2] Maybe you've even heard it said that God is with us.[3] These are all true, but God is also Jesus, and God is also the Holy Spirit. One of the most mysterious wonders of God is that He exists in three distinct persons: The Father, The Son, and The Holy Spirit. This is The Trinity.

THE SON

"So the Word became human and made his home among us."

— JOHN 1:14, NLT

As magnificent as nature is, God opens our eyes to see Him in an even more incredible way through Jesus Christ. God came to earth in the body of Jesus Christ over two thousand years ago in the ancient land of Israel. Jesus was conceived in the womb of an unwed, teenaged woman named Mary. Through God's supernatural favour, Mary was touched by His Holy Spirit and became pregnant. Jesus was born in Bethlehem and lived most of His life in Nazareth, working alongside His step-dad as a carpenter. At the age of thirty, He began to teach, heal, and pour out unconditional love to all who encountered Him. Jesus was seen by the eyes of thousands during His thirty-three years on earth, including a widow with two coins, a bleeding woman, a crooked woman, a woman at a well, a demon-possessed Mary, a young daughter, plus many more.

Jesus did something dramatic in the last three years of His life, and it was too much for the people back then; He began to proclaim He was God. This is what finally got Him killed. He wasn't just a great teacher, healer, and prophet. Jesus was God's very own Son, fully human and fully God, with the divine purpose to bring all of us back into a right relationship with God.

THE HOLY SPIRIT

Once Jesus' purpose was fulfilled on earth, He went back to be with God, but He didn't leave us all alone after doing the beautiful work of making us right with God. Instead, He sent someone to journey with us – the Holy Spirit. This incredible divine Person is a gift from Jesus so we would never be without His presence and power. I'm going to write about the Holy Spirit later, but for now, think of Him as a wonderful guide who prepares us to meet Jesus.

TRULY INVISIBLE INSIDE OF US

Every single woman reading this book can experience God in her life. When a person becomes a follower of Jesus, all three Persons of the Trinity take up residence in them, and their spirit comes alive. God is the only person who can do this for us. Nobody else.

Here's where your part comes into play. God won't do anything in you without your permission. This makes sense because, as I've mentioned a few times, God is a gentleman. He has given every one of us our own free-will to do whatever we want to do. He can't come into your heart if you hate Him and want nothing to do with Him or if your intentions are to continue down your dark path of destruction.

Jesus is The Invisible God inside of us, when we agree to let Him in.

> *"But to all who believed him and accepted him, he gave the right to become children of God. They are reborn—not with a physical birth resulting from human passion or plan, but a birth that comes from God."*
>
> — JOHN 1:12-13, NLT

PRAY

I believe we are ready to invite Him in when we come to a place in our life where we want change so much that we cry out, "Oh change me, please. I don't want to live like this anymore. There has to be a better way. Is this all there is? There has to be something more than this."

Instead of hopelessness, the Invisible God gives us hope of a different way. This way is through Jesus Christ. These simple words can be your prayer to Him today:

> *"I want to change. I know I have done many things in my life that are destructive to me and others, and I want to change this. I can't seem to do this on my own, so, Jesus, would You help me? Take my heart and my life, and change them. I can't see You, but I'm trusting You are there and that You will help me. I am looking for a better way to live my life. Thank You. Amen."*

SOMETHING TO PONDER

Another sure way to see the unseen God is through people. When we look into the eyes of a hurting person, a homeless woman, an anxiety-ridden teenager, a broken-hearted widow, a sad nephew hiding behind jokes, or a depressed co-worker, we can actually see Jesus there looking back at us.

May I suggest taking time to ponder and remember this because at some point in our own shattered lives somebody looked into our sad, troubled eyes and saw Jesus there. They embraced us and shared the news of His wonderful love. Hallelujah.

> *"No one has ever seen God; but if we love one another, God lives in us and his love is made complete in us."*
>
> — 1 JOHN 4:12, NIV

THE CATCHING GOD AND THE CAUGHT WOMAN

"However softly we speak, God is near enough to hear us."
— Teresa of Ávila —

"I lift up my eyes to the hills – where does my help come from? My help comes from the LORD, the Maker of Heaven and earth. He will not let your foot slip – he who watches over you will not slumber. Indeed, he who watches over Israel will neither slumber nor sleep. The LORD watches over you – the LORD is your shade at your right hand; the sun will not harm you by day nor the moon by night. The LORD will keep you from all harm – he will watch over your life; the LORD will watch over your coming and going both now and forevermore."
— Psalm 121, NIV —

$\mathscr{P}$salm 121 is poetic, protective, hopeful, and promising and my favourite psalm. God isn't looking to see what I am up to in any one day, shaking His head when I do or say something stupid. Instead, He is watching over and protecting me forever, not only from evil but from the mistakes I make.

I want to share the major shame story from my life which changed everything for me. This event tied the bloodiest knots in my heart and took years to untie. But for the grace of God, it would have destroyed me.

At sixteen, I found myself pregnant. I thought I'd better see a doctor after a few months with no period, so I made an appointment for myself and went alone without telling my mom. Our family didn't talk much, so I had trouble talking with her, especially about this. After my examination, I sat in the chair opposite the doctor, and he confirmed I was pregnant. *Now what?* He asked me what I wanted to do. I blurted out: "I don't want to have it."

"I can arrange for you to go to the hospital and have it taken out, but you need to bring your mom in to sign the papers." It was that easy in the mid 1970s. His words were life changing.

I managed to tell my mom in a cowardly way by putting a hand-written note of confession into her purse. She was heading to the grocery store and stopped at the kitchen counter digging through her purse for her keys when she found it. She was certainly disappointed in me, but when I cried, she hugged me while I blubbered about how scared I was. She questioned me about the boy, but I didn't reveal any details about this to her. It didn't matter; it wasn't a case of getting married and living happily ever after or anything like that. I didn't have a steady boyfriend. I had made a rather large mistake: I brought this pregnancy home with me after living on the streets in a resort town during that one free and wild summer I mentioned in the previous chapter.

The following weeks led to a folding in of myself driven by shame for what I had done and the choices I had made. We went to the next doctor's appointment together and the adults spoke as if I wasn't in the room. Invisible. The thing I remember the most during the appointment was my mom's comments to the doctor: "Well, this isn't going to be on her record as an abortion, is it?" *My record? Like a criminal?* I guess in a sense I was.

Mom and I were in a private room at the hospital when we heard footsteps coming down the hallway that sounded similar to the stomping footsteps of her new mother-in-law.

"That bloody well sounds like Gertie. That's all I need—to get caught here with you in this situation. How would I explain any of this mess? I'll never hear the end of it." She got up and closed the door. Gertie (the mother of my mom's new husband) was in fact in the hospital visiting her dying husband—at the same time I was there for an abortion.

What I needed the most from my mom in this situation was a hug and some compassion. Instead I experienced insignificance and shame for being a dirty daughter with a dirty affliction; the new mother-in-law was much more important than I was.

The operation happened, and I was sent home the next day. When I was picked up, there were no hugs, no words of: "It'll be okay; we'll get through this." There were no bedside chats, no offered affection. Nobody held me in their arms and sobbed with me. Nobody brought me a hot cup of tea in bed and said, "Just rest a bit. I love you." No kindness or compassion was given. No grace.

I grieved terribly for this loss, but I didn't know how deeply until my stepfather said to me one night through his drunken, half-closed eyes, "I hear you crying yourself to sleep every night for what you've done." No compassion or comfort there either.

I had nobody to talk with at home, so I met up with a friend a few days later and told her what happened. Her response wasn't what I wanted to hear.

"Did you get to see it?"

"Did I get to see what?"

"The fetus."

Was there anybody with any sense of compassion for what I had gone through? There wasn't a program in place nor a guidance counsellor at school to help girls through this kind of trauma in the mid '70s. And how would my mother ever bring this secret up to anybody so I could be helped? She couldn't. Didn't. I decided I was on my own. *It's true then—nobody does love me.*

When I finally went back to school, I wandered the hallways from class to class in a daze. I had folded into myself so drastically; I became a teenager without any friends. This was one of the loneliest times in my life. When lunchtime came, I wandered the school grounds alone, waiting for the bell to ring so I had someplace to go, or I walked aimlessly up and down the hallways, avoiding everyone I knew.

I would sit quietly in the classroom and fade into anonymity, listening, taking notes, and coping as best I could with the trauma. I had changed from being amongst a group of chattering teenage girls to a nobody—all alone in only a matter of a few weeks.

I plummeted from being an honour roll student to dropping out of high school a few months later. I left home nine months after that and moved away to a city I had never been to with $150 in my pocket. Heck, I had never been more than one hundred miles away from where I grew up, but still, I ran away as soon as I could from all of them—my family, friends, relatives, and teachers. I was just so lost.

The abortion was never spoken of again by anybody just as if it never happened. Not a word. It was a dark secret. I didn't even speak of it myself because that's the way it was in my family. The only time I ever mentioned it to my mom was in a letter when I was unsuccessful in getting pregnant in my first marriage and wondered how long I would have to pay for the horrible thing I had done.

A word of love would have been good. A touch of compassion would have been healing. A measure of empathy would have eased my self-hatred. A heart reaching out towards me would have given me a sense of hope when there wasn't any at all. But that wasn't the way things were done in the house I grew up in. Emotions—what were they? What in the world were kind words? Nobody asked me how I felt. Nobody wanted to hear. How I wish I had met Jesus back then for the sake of my sixteen-year-old self.

"Let him kiss me...."

— SONG OF SONGS 1:2, NIV

In the aftermath of all this, I ended up believing the lies placed in my head through the words I'd heard and magazine articles I'd read that I would be punished for having an abortion. I believed the consequences were that I would never have children of my own. The gift of motherhood was never given to me, and in two marriages, no children were born.

When I came under the loving wings of Jesus, all of my wrongdoings were wiped out, including this one. No longer do I believe the lie that the reason I didn't have any children was punishment for the teenage mistake I had made. The sins of abortion and the shame of it are gone and taken away by Him forever. I am no longer condemned.

I will let You kiss me...

STICKS AND STONES MAY BREAK MY BONES

Jesus loves women, so He brings hope and freedom to us. This should be the best news you've ever heard. This should be comforting news for women living under the black cloud of shame. I don't need to explain shame to most women because the majority of us have experienced it.

Shame stings and throbs. Shame beats on in a dull pain, always steering us towards an unloved life, tearing apart our tender hearts and minds, destroying what value we may have for ourselves. Shame devours us and twists the way we see ourselves. We learn to live with our shame glasses on, feeling worthless and unlovable. We are either not good enough the way we are, or we are way over the top in our emotions. Either way, we feel ashamed for those emotions and tears or for what we seemingly can't bring to the table: our shortcomings, our weaknesses, our deep-seated feelings of "never good enough."

I recall a time in my life when I was at my second lowest place. I had just left my ex-husband, finally escaping a toxic marriage which I'd helped to create. Do you ever get horrible nightmares about somebody you are living with? I had many at the end of this marriage, which I believe were warnings from God to leave.

In those terrifying nightmares, a blackness rose out of me with pointing fingers and a screaming roar towards the man in the bed with me, my ex-husband. Why do I believe these were a warning from God? I never experienced another nightmare once I was away from him and living elsewhere. God is always good, and He has compassion for all He has made. Praise God for this.

I was finally on my own, away from him at last, but I was shattered all the same. In the end, it doesn't matter who wants the divorce; it's still a failed marriage with a devastating loss. Many tears were shed while I lay awake on that basement pullout couch, hiding in the dark in emotional turmoil.

Could life be any bleaker than this? When I couldn't stand myself any longer, I would go to a girlfriend's house and sleep on her couch in the living room curled up in a ball. One night when I was in the most tearful and inconsolable stage she said, "I thought you were a lot stronger than this. Get it together." I stopped crying; these words stung. The implication that I was a pathetic weakling and shouldn't need to bleed any longer filled my soul with more shame—again.

There is no doubt I was falling apart, and my emotional state was over the top, but... A hug, a hot cup of tea, and permission to cry some more would have been so much better than more condemnation and rejection.

Shame comes to us in ways not always simple and sometimes without intention, but it seems shame almost always comes by way of the spoken word.

Sticks and stone will break my bones, but words can never harm me.

Who hasn't heard this consoling piece of advice from one of our parents while growing up? We came home in tears after the school bully yelled cruel words in the schoolyard and got this advice: "Well, the next time he taunts you, you just tell him that 'sticks and stone will break my bones but words can never harm me.'" There, all better now.

This verse is actually an old children's rhyme used to deter name calling and bullying, and its roots go back to the 1800s. The African Methodist Episcopal Church published it in one of their publications of *The Christian Recorder* in March 1862.[1]

The truth is that words can be the most hurtful weapons of all. Verbal abuse is devastating. It's enough we have so many of our own terrifying thoughts running around our minds telling us how ugly, fat, or stupid we are—surely, we don't need somebody else's words, too. What we need are the words of Jesus.

THE WOMAN CAUGHT IN ADULTERY

"Jesus straightened up and asked her, "Woman, where are they? Has no one condemned you?" "No one, sir," she said. "Then neither do I condemn you," Jesus declared. "Go now and leave your life of sin."

— JOHN 8:10-11, NIV

The woman in John 8 was dragged in front of the crowd at the temple (where all the "good" people were) and was shamed by words of accusation. There is no accusing without the use of hurtful, devilish, and dark words. Words have the power to build up and to tear down. *Look what this dirty woman has done. Can you believe it? Just look at her. Filthy. Unclean.*

She was caught in an adulterous affair, perhaps a one-night stand. She may have been set up by the self-righteous temple leaders as a way to discredit and trap Jesus in His understanding of the law. Whatever the circumstances were, she was thrown in front of a hostile crowd, all alone, while everyone gawked, hoping for some drama and excitement.

I can imagine they hissed at her, spit in her face, calling her all sorts of cruel names as they laughed at her when she was pushed to the ground. Stoning was the price for adultery in this ancient culture—a fatal consequence. Did the law only apply to women back then? No, it didn't, so where was the man?[2] He was nowhere to be found—she stood alone.

Her accusers pointed fingers and hurled violent words at her, heaping more and more shame upon her as she stood there shaking. And look at what Jesus did. He bent down to write something in the dust. Some scholars believe he wrote verses from Scripture, commandments, and some believe He wrote the names of all the men standing around facing her with a rock in their hands.

We will never know what He wrote in the dust, and I don't think we really need to know because His loving actions defending her are enough to heal our broken hearts of feeling guilty and ashamed. Jesus stood back up and asked the men who were ready to pummel her with stones: *"If any of you is without sin, let him be the first to throw a stone at her"* (John 8:7, NIV). Then He stooped back down and wrote in the dust once more.

This is brilliant. Jesus loves us women. Nobody heaved a stone at her. Instead they snuck away—the old men leaving first. Why do the older men leave first? It gets mentioned in the story so it must have significance. (Everything mentioned in the Bible has purpose.)

Here's an idea or two. It seems to me that, as people age, they either get nicer or nastier. For some people, nothing seems overly important anymore except for matters of the heart, and so they become nicer, gentler people with soft, open hearts. On the other hand, for some people, everything becomes exceedingly important and inflexible with an *"it's my way or the highway"* attitude; their hearts continue to harden and become further closed to everything and everyone.

Perhaps these older men standing with rocks in their hands realized how hypocritical they were, having had affairs of their own with a woman just like the one in the middle of their vicious circle—they knew they should be standing in her place. Could it be that their hearts were opened with compassion for her in the presence of Jesus, and they fled, embarrassed by their frenzied participation in bullying this woman? Or maybe they came to the conclusion they had so many more sins piled up against them and were never going to be forgiven, so they fled in fear thinking, *I'd better get out of here, or I'm next!* Whatever the case may be, when Jesus stood back up again, nobody was there except the woman.

> *"'Has no one condemned you?' 'No one.' 'Then neither do I condemn you. Go now and leave your life of sin.'"*
>
> — JOHN 8:10-11, NIV

Jesus showed such mercy and grace to this woman who was shamed in front of the whole town she lived in. The story doesn't tell us what happened to her afterwards, but I think she did change her ways. She had been touched by Jesus, so how could she ever be the same again? I know I wasn't. Her life had been returned to her. As a precious, darling daughter of God, heaps of value, significance, and worth were poured upon her. This is God's grace. We don't deserve His favour, but He gives it to us anyway.

I was caught in teenage pregnancy and abortion. This woman was caught in adultery. No matter who we think we are, we are bound to get caught in our immorality sooner or later. Sins are sins, so I'm going to call them sins instead of some other word for the wrongs we do in our lives (like excuses, mistakes, or troubles) because it's all the same. We all seem to get caught sooner or later; the sooner the better actually because then we can be forgiven and get set free.

Don't you want this freedom and forgiveness for your life? Aren't you sick and tired of lying to your family? Cheating on your husband? Closet drinking? Spending your paycheck on clothes you can't afford? Stealing from your employer?

Yes, absolutely, I had to ask for forgiveness for taking a life through an abortion. I probably needed to do this more than anybody else because I didn't think I'd done anything wrong.

My life is better this way.

I had to acknowledge and confess how terrible this operation truly was, as well as my obtuse attitude towards it, even though I was a teenager at the time. He created a life in me, and I ended it—a sin against God.

THE CATCHING GOD

One night, I dreamed of sitting on a rock on a cliff's edge with my feet dangling over it. The rock was smooth, cream-coloured, well-worn, and polished. *Have I been sitting here so long this stone has worn smooth under me? Probably, or God wouldn't be bringing it to my attention in a dream.*

In my dream, I decided I wanted off the seat. There was a problem however—I couldn't stand up. There was no place to set my foot to power myself up, and likewise, there was nothing to grab onto with my hands to pull myself up. I needed leverage where there wasn't any. The cliff was too steep, and the seat was too smooth. *He's right, of course. I've been sitting here way too long—in the shame seat, living the small life, the life I was never meant to live, accepting things the way they are, never flying.*

It became clear that the only way off the seat was to jump off the cliff and fly. *Jump into the air and fly?* Yes, fly!

Right into His arms. Right into the life He had always planned for me. *Isn't this beautiful? Isn't this scary? Isn't this glorious? To fly. Into freedom. Into the arms of the One who planned me and everything for me even before my mother fell in love with my earthly father.*

Are you sitting in the seat of shame and living a small life? Or are you sitting on a seat owned by somebody else as you seek their approval in everything? Do you want to get off this cliff-side seat and fly? Ask Jesus to catch you because you've had enough of your safe, mediocre life, and now you want to fly. Even if you're living a life full of non-stop drama, it's still a safe, mediocre life because you know it well—you made it after all, so it's easy to remain there.

It can be scary for some women to give up their life of non-stop drama. For me, the scary step was saying yes to doing something I swore as a young girl I would never ever do again, which was going back into a church where all the "good" people were. Saying yes and taking a powerful and clear stand, banging my hand upon the table and saying: "This is what I know to be true! There is one truth. Jesus died for me so I could have a better life. The least I can do is claim it."

Most recently, my scary step was saying yes to writing this book for Him. Our steps—big, small, scary, or bold—are so pleasing to Jesus.

If you really want to change your life, jump off your smooth, polished seat and fly into The Catching God's arms. Trust completely that He will catch you—this is another loving characteristic of the Almighty God. He is trustworthy and faithful. We can trust Him with our life one hundred percent because He gave it to us, and He knows every single day of it. And He provided a way for us to live our life abundantly and joyfully, which is with Him. Jesus is The Catching God who will catch you as you leap off the cliff's edge into His loving, safe, everlasting arms. He will catch you.

GOD WANTS YOU

God wants you to embrace the life you have, just like He wants me to embrace the life I have without children or grandchildren. He knows it is not ideal what has happened to you, but it happened. Search for the beauty in the ashes of your mistakes, and don't guilt yourself out any longer with lies about you deserving some sort of punishment.

The loneliness, shame, darkness and depression are enough to bear, and God knows all about your suffering. He has been there throughout your whole life, ready to catch you when you have fallen. Your life is a divine story which He has planned for you from the very beginning.

If only you would have recognized Him sooner, Jesus would have taken the pain and suffering away sooner, but perhaps you were not ready. Maybe you were stubborn on your feet, trying to show the world you were bold and brave. He wants you to give up the shame and unhappiness concerning your situation and instead embrace the truth that He sees you as His lovely, forgiven daughter. You will never be lonely, unloved, shamed, condemned, afraid, or hopeless again when you accept Him into your life.

It is not difficult to believe in Jesus when there is such hopelessness in the world, and it is getting more hopeless as the years go by. To the women who feel unloved, abandoned and outcast, He doesn't hate you, and He hasn't left you alone; instead He loves you and will never leave you.

There is hope in your life. There is love to be nurtured and grown. There is beauty in the ashes of your messes to be discovered, and there is a plan and purpose for your life if you will let Jesus love you and allow Him access to your life.

God is waiting for your invitation. He wants your *yes,* but He also wants to forgive you for all the big and little mistakes you've made in your life. They will be forgiven but not forgotten because some things we can't simply forget. He wants you to ask for forgiveness because He can't help you with the damaged areas until you agree and admit to your part in them. This might be "jumping off the cliff" for you— scary but necessary if you are ever going to fly.

TRULY CATCHING

These are words God spoke into my writing one day for this book:

> *I am their Catching God. I will catch every woman who is going to go through what you did. I will never forsake them, even if they don't want Me right now—like you did. They are mine and I will never leave them. You must tell them this. I want every woman to know there is a way out of their ashes. It is easy, and it is with Me. She needs to know there is no shame in the pain she has gone through. She doesn't need to feel or live with shame anymore. She just needs to turn away from her messed up ways, say yes to Me, and let Me love her.*

PRAY

> *Lord, I am beginning to believe the only help I can truly count on comes from You and that You are always watching over me. I've had enough of this mediocre life I am living, and I've had enough of the drama, too. Please open up Your arms and catch me. Please don't let me go. Please take the shame and the pain away, and let me come alive in You. Thank you, Jesus. Amen.*

SOMETHING TO PONDER

What would it take for you to say yes to jumping off your safe seat and flying into the trusting and loving arms of The Catching God? Where does your help come from?

And when He catches you, thank Him, will you?

> "Look at you, my dearest darling, you are so lovely! You are beauty itself to me."
>
> — SONG OF SONGS 1:15, NIV

THE UNSTOPPABLE GOD AND THE
WIDOW OF NAIN

"The world has an awful beauty. This is a chaotic place,
humanity is a chaotic place, and I am a chaotic place."[1]
— Anne Lamott —

*"But then I will win her back once again. I will lead her into the desert
and speak tenderly to her there. I will return her vineyards to her and
transform the Valley of Trouble into a gateway of hope."*
— Hosea 2:14-15, NLT —

*I*s there hope in the valley of my own, self-made trouble?

How did God make Himself known to me when I had no
fatherly relationship to relate to, no spiritual connection, and no
desire to get to know God in the first place? I was doing everything
but looking for God in my life, and still He pursued me until I was
curious about Him. But He let me get to the bottom of myself first—a
desert place.

He knows the place we each have to get to before we will cry out at
our wit's end for His help. Maybe the desert place for you is sitting in
a detox center or an abortion clinic. Maybe it's getting home to your

husband after sleeping with somebody else. Did you shop all day at the mall, spending money on clothes you can't afford only to shove them to the back of the closet to keep them hidden from your spouse? Did you get high all weekend, and now you're at work, having one last snort in the bathroom before heading to your desk?

Are you simply tired of all the emptiness and sadness inside, where nothing brings you any joy? Maybe this is the desert place for you.

I consumed all sorts of "bad medicine" to fill up my empty soul, the missing part deep inside of me. Every time listened to Bonnie Raitt sing her song "Guilty," I'd get choked up because the lyrics described my life and heart back then. They went something like this: I'm gonna need a whole lot of medicine to keep on pretending I'm somebody else. That was me!

LET THE PARTY BEGIN

I was off to the city to land a job in an office—with a real boss, and letterhead, and filing cabinets. I had grand dreams of lounging on a chaise lounge, draped in a satin gown, and smoking a cigarette in a fancy holder because I was going to be making so much money as a receptionist. Nobody told me most of my paycheque would go to a landlord and the rest to the grocery store. *So much for the gown and cigarette holder.*

No sooner had I landed the job, I met an older man, and we moved in together. It turned out, the first man I would have a serious relationship with was a drinker and a womanizer. This relationship lasted about a year and a half until I was so miserable, I couldn't take another day with him, so I left. I moved into a house with a few girls and found a new job. I was twenty and the party was on for the next decade or so.

I met girls at my new job who were just like me: young, silly, and experimenting with everything we could get our hands on, believing we were pretty cool and sexy. We drank lots of alcohol, spent many hours in dark nightclubs smoking cigarettes and of course pot.

Speed? Sure. Cocaine? Yes, indeed—especially cocaine. We laughed a lot, but we threw up a lot, too. We chased men everywhere we went, and if they were bad boys, they were all the more attractive to us. The bad guys were usually men with drugs or enough money to buy them.

At twenty-three I married a man whom I'd met one summer through friends. We partied well together and fell in love (I guess). It was the 1980s, and everything was big and excessive then—the hair, the cars, the drinks, the padded shoulders, the business lunches, and the credit card debt. The drugs were just as big, too, and we experimented with MDA and cocaine, just like the crowd we were hanging out with. During all this madness, I held down a job, tried to keep a house, and got a puppy.

I should have seen the first signs right away, but I didn't clue in for a long time. After three months of marriage, he didn't come home one weekend. He spent it at his brother's house partying. He was afraid he'd made a big mistake getting married—his brother explained to me, trying to patch things up on his behalf. This was the first lie, but it happened again soon enough.

This would be the pattern of our marriage for the next ten years.

After a few years, I got tired of the partying and wanted a different life. I'd had enough of the drugs and the wasted weekends. I was beginning to change but not fast enough.

I left him after five years but returned when he showed up one night at my apartment crying and asking me to come back home where I belonged. I wasn't quite done yet, so I returned for another five years. I missed my sweet dog - which I had left behind - so terribly, so I was easily convinced to go back and try again. I wanted somebody, anybody, to love me, and I hadn't found it yet.

We bought a house and some nice, new wine glasses. A new car and furniture should help, right? We went on a few vacations. Every few weeks, he'd come home drunk or wouldn't come home at all.

Then the "wrong number" phone calls began and continued throughout our marriage. When I was finally gone for good, I realized other households didn't get "wrong numbers" all the time. One night, a "wrong number" described what my husband did for her.

He began to call me names, unattractive and shameful names that hurt. He said none of his friends or family liked me. Those words were not what I wanted to hear since I wore "nobody loves me" quite well. His lies got bigger. His nights away became more frequent, and I began to experience horrific nightmares. Then I started jogging. Was running the equivalent of scrubbing walls? Probably.

Let me point my finger back to myself so you don't think, "Oh, you poor thing," and that I was completely innocent in this marriage. I wasn't. I partied, too. I did drugs, too. The worst thing I did was have an affair. I skulked around just like all the other adulterers who chase the thrill of sex with somebody they aren't married to. The affair was exciting at the time until I got inside the door of my home. Then it turned into shame and disappointment. I ended up hating myself. I was to blame for the mess just as much as he was.

Eventually, I came up with the "big idea" to fix everything: If I could just have a baby, maybe everything would get better. I wanted some-body to love me, and I wanted to love somebody back; a baby would fix all my problems. He couldn't have children, so I began to explore alternative methods of conceiving and went through many months of artificial means but without result.

I received a doctor's letter during this time with a prescription inside for STD's; it took this letter to finally hit home that I wasn't in the same marriage as he was. It got worse, but I don't need to tell any more stories... You get the picture. It was going to be a long journey to crawl out of the destruction, confusion, and the deceit I had helped to create.

SOMETHING HAS TO CHANGE

I didn't have much wisdom back then, only the pain and shame and a growing knowledge that something was really wrong with the way I was living. Something had to change. Where did this desire for change come from? I wanted to love someone and to have someone love me back. Was this too much to ask for? I didn't consider there might be a God who loves me. I didn't want Him.

Yet God was thinking of me. He never stopped working on me—after all, He created me and knew exactly how to allure me to Him. We can see the hand of God in our lives easily when we look backwards, not forwards. At the time, I didn't think God had any part of my life, but today I know He protected me during this season of my life. I believe He didn't allow a baby to be born into a bad marriage. Lovingly, He sent me a huge message with the nightmares to show me it was time to move on. Later, through my ex-husband's boss, I met a young woman named Kathleen, all as planned. The Unstoppable God was continually watching over me while I stumbled around hoping to find love—which in the end, is Him.

FROM MY DIARY

I'm sharing an entry from my journal written during my desert time in the basement. It's dark with a small glimmer of hope at the end where God begins to call me.

Sometimes I feel so worthless and I hate myself so much. I can daydream and click off so easily it's frightening. And I can honestly say I don't know how to relate to people—like I have a real problem communicating and feeling safe with anybody. It's like a building block is missing—like I missed something somewhere. I can't relate, and I've never fit in with anybody. I felt I fit in with the people at work when I was 20-21, but we were all drinking and doing drugs so much. We partied and partied. But since then, I just don't fit in. WHY!!?? What is wrong with me? Some more negatives… It seems I never finish anything I start—like night school courses, etc. I'm afraid of my success, so I quit—like high school. I have more compassion and empathy for animals than I do for humans. I'm terrified of the spiritual or religious field. I've always and still do feel guilty about everything I do. I feel guilty if I stop a car when I walk across a street, I feel guilty like for such stupid things. I feel guilty ALWAYS!!!! I'm sorry—I can't think of any good things about myself except my independence. I've never felt like I needed anyone. I feel like I could become a recluse and never talk to anybody again. I just don't feel like anybody's ever liked me enough to make me feel like they need me or I need them. I don't need anybody in this world. I feel like the loneliest person in the world tonight. I just don't feel strong anymore. I feel like I could die and it wouldn't matter to anybody or anything at all! Just to go to sleep and never wake up would be blissful, never having to feel bad again and never having to feel again. I hate myself!!! I can't stop crying, and I put on this front that cracks so easily. I am all alone and nobody gives a ------. What is all this about anyways. Why am I here? WHY?? Oh, I am so black inside at times and in such pain. I wish this life was over. It just keeps getting worse and worse. BUT a little voice inside whispers to me "That's sad." I do need people—I don't want to have a lonely life.

In hearing other people's stories, I notice we seem to all reach a certain place which triggers us to cry out for even the dullest of lights to shine in us. I don't know what it is for you, but you'll know, and Jesus already knows. He is just waiting for you to say these small, yet powerful, words:

Jesus, please help me.

The desert place was the only place where I actually listened to God. Why not just talk to me sweetly where I was? He tried, but I wasn't listening, so it was in these dark times where He finally got my attention. It was up to me to actually listen.

I discovered I needed to be saved from myself because, as it turns out, I couldn't do it for myself—I tried. Instead of untying those bloodied knots of shame, fear, worthlessness, and insecurity that were clogging up my heart, I kept tying them tighter and tighter. I needed Someone supernatural to untie them for me.

A WORLD WITHOUT HOPE

Everyone needs hope in their life. What is hope anyway?

I hope you're feeling better.

Hope you're having a great day.

Gee, I hope this paint colour matches my duvet.

I really hope he likes me.

I hope my car starts or I'm hooped.

I hope I'm not getting sick again.

Fingers crossed, I hope I get that promotion at work.

Hope you have a great birthday (anniversary, wedding, operation, fill in the blank…).

I've been noticing how often I use this word but in a meaningless, pedestrian way—watered down. Look at all the ways I've used it here as an example. It doesn't appear to carry any strong meaning at all in these instances. It often just becomes a way to emphasize or pass on a thought, or even to help us feel better about ourselves. Lately, it seems the world is without any hope whatsoever.

What does hope *really* mean?

The meaning of hope in Dictionary.com reads like this:

> "the feeling that what is wanted can be had or that events will turn out for the best, a particular instance of this feeling; to look forward to with desire and reasonable confidence; to believe, desire, or trust; to feel that something desired may happen; to place trust; rely."[2]

Yes, hope is one thing our world desperately needs.

What does the Bible say about hope? I think the whole, lovely, beautiful Bible is a book of hope. It promises: *"Three things will last forever— faith, hope, and love—and the greatest of these is love"* (1 Corinthians 13:13, NLT). Hope is right up there with love and will last forever. We aren't going to be left alone to die in our sorrow and darkness after all. We get to go home and live with God in the end, and He assures us a special place when we get there.

God has given us a beautiful landing spot in eternity with this promise from Jesus: *"My Father's house has many dwelling places. If it were otherwise, I would tell you plainly, because I go to prepare a place for you to rest"* (John 14:2, TPT). It's not the world we live in right now that our hearts and souls ache for—it's eternity with Him.

Spiritual hope, then, is something different than this pedestrian hope we so often refer to. Spiritual hope is the strong desire to connect with God and a longing to be with Him in our future.

It's what we are made for. When we make a choice to believe in Jesus and follow Him, spiritual hope is ours.

THE WIDOW OF NAIN

> *"When the Lord saw her, His heart went out to her, and He said, "Don't cry."*
>
> — LUKE 7:13, NLT

Can you hear His love and compassion in these few words? I can.

The story of the Widow of Nain is a loving, grace-filled story in Scripture about a vulnerable woman without hope. She lived in the village of Nain south of Nazareth where Jesus grew up. He had just finished teaching on a mountainside to large crowds of hungry people, who wanted to hear some hope for themselves. He had begun to reveal to the crowd who He really was by a miraculous healing of a military leader's servant in Capernaum.

He traveled down to Nain with his disciples after these events, and He noticed a funeral procession as they got near to the town. There was wailing, moaning, and crying for a young man who had died; the attendants were taking his body to his final burial place outside the town.

She was a widow. This is an integral part of the story. Jewish women during this time in history didn't have jobs to support themselves. They relied on the men in their lives, so if you had a husband, you ate, and if you had a son, you ate. When her husband died, she had no means to support herself except through her son, so she most likely moved into his household. Now, she had lost her son, too. What would become of her? Would she end up selling herself as a prostitute or a slave in order to feed herself? That was certainly a possibility.

I can picture the scene with crowds of people following a coffin and her walking beside her dead son, weeping. It was dry and hot out as they walked along. Some people in the crowd had been paid to wail and mourn (a Jewish funeral tradition). Did these paid mourners make up most of the crowd? I wonder if she had any friends or family left at all to help her. Would she be tossed aside, left to scramble for food, and to somehow find a way to survive? Did she lose all hope when she lost her only son?

Jesus saw her stumbling along beside the coffin, weeping. The Bible says *"His heart overflowed with compassion"* (Luke 7:13, NLT). Why? Because He loved her. Not only did He say something to her to ease her sorrow and bring her comfort, but He performed a miracle. She didn't ask for this. She didn't say a word to him.

Did she even know who Jesus was? He was with a crowd of men and women walking along the road, but so what? There were lots of spiritual leaders walking around the countryside in those days with crowds following behind. He's just another one. Except He wasn't just another one. He did something nobody else had done, and He did it in front of a wailing crowd of onlookers, giving hope to this widow.

He saw how deeply wounded she was and knew her future would be bleak without her son around. Was Jesus also seeing into the future of his own mother, Mary, and sympathizing with the suffering she would be facing shortly when he died on the cross? Perhaps.

He leaned over the coffin and touched it, telling the dead man to arise and get up. There was a moment of silence when everyone and everything seemed to be suspended as they waited for something to happen. Or were they all gasping because He was bothering to help a lowly woman, thinking, "Well, this just isn't right"? For Jesus to be speaking with this woman was a blatant breaking of the societal rules, and to help a woman by performing a miracle on her life—that was simply earth-shattering.

The young man arose and did a strange thing—he started talking right away. This is an interesting point to the story because the widow hasn't said a word through this whole encounter, but the dead man who comes alive speaks up right away. They've all witnessed a supernatural miracle right before their eyes, and to make it even more impactful, the young man was healed so completely from death that he is able to speak right away.

Jesus brought her son back to life and, in a sense, brought her life back to life, too. This is grace. God's kindness. Now she is alive with the gift of hope and a prosperous future. Hope comes alive when we are touched by the heart of Jesus. Everyone who allows Jesus to touch their life has a beautiful future ahead.

THE UNSTOPPABLE GOD

The Unstoppable God never gives up on me. The promises of God always remind me that he wants me and has chosen me. I tell myself, *If God chose me and had a plan for me all along then it only makes logical sense He would never give up on me.* God chose you, too. How many of you feel left out, excluded? In the secular world, millions and millions of women are excluded, but with God, everyone is included—this is the beauty of God's story. If you really want to change your life, believe God wants you and has chosen you.

I am God's chosen daughter. I'm a princess! I live with His crown upon my head, promising me a better mind, heart, soul, and attitude as well as a better story. I live with the hope of eternity in my heart. This is what I was made for.

At some point you might want to make a decision to live differently from the life you've created for yourself. You can be sure that if you do, God has a better story for you as well.

NEVER STOPS PURSUING

My story is evidence enough for me to believe that He will never stop working on me. It is why I believe He is The Unstoppable God. He has shown me He will never stop pursuing and loving me. He will never stop communicating with me. He will never stop blessing me. He will never stop providing for me. He will never stop alluring me and speaking tenderly to me. He will never stop protecting me.

He knows that His presence is the best place for me to be, and He wants me to know this, too. This sacred place near Him is where our divine story and adventure takes place, so He won't stop prompting us until we claim it.

I want to be near Him always, feeling His breath on my face. The smell of Him, the touch of Him, the colours of Him—He settles my raging soul. His peace unravels my tied-up heart.

He brings rest to my chaotic mind with whispers to my heart:

> *O Child of Mine, settle down. Take My breath breathed into you.*
> *Take My peace, take My heart, take My love, take what I offer you,*
> *and rest in Me.*

PRAY

> *Jesus, things seem to be hopeless for me at times, and I can't seem to*
> *change on my own. I want to be happy instead of sad all the time. I*
> *need You to help me. My life can be messy at times, and I'm so tired of*
> *the mess. Please don't stop loving me and helping me. Take away this*
> *knotted-up heart of mine and replace it with a new one. I want to*
> *experience life closer to You. Thank You that You pursue me and*
> *never give up on me, even though I give up on myself at times. Thank*
> *You that You do all these things because You love me. Amen.*

Remember, He doesn't want fancy, complicated words—just simple ones from your lovely heart.

SOMETHING TO PONDER

Do you have hope in your life? Do you want to live a life filled with hope? Do you believe God wants to have a relationship with you? Do you believe in eternity?

> *"But as for me, it is good to be near God."*

— PSALM 73:28, NIV

THE ILLUMINATING GOD AND THE TRAVELING WOMEN

"I am the light of the world."
— John 8:12, NIV —

*"For God, who said, "Let there be light in the darkness,"
has made this light shine in our hearts so we could know
the glory of God that is seen in the face of Jesus Christ."*
— 2 Corinthians 4:5, NLT —

I'm an ordinary woman. I haven't had an extreme experience of spiritual conversion like God speaking to me from a burning bush type of thing, but here's the strange thing—I *want* to go to church nowadays and I *want* to know more about Him. I *want* to know the truth. What's more is I *want* to sing songs, worshipping God. Yet I didn't have a huge conversion experience. It wasn't like that for me. This *wanting* is God's way of continually drawing me towards Himself, enticing me to follow His Son and be more like Him. I now understand God has used everything from my past to attract me to Himself—exactly as He has always wanted it to be.

God the Father has a different plan and way with each one of us. He didn't save me the same way He saved some of my sisters and brothers or the way He will save you. He saved me the only way I would respond. He illuminated the way for me before I even knew I was being called.

THE TRAVELING WOMEN

During Jesus' ministry years, there were women who accompanied Him and His disciples from place to place. Who were these women who traveled around the Galilean countryside with Jesus? They were ordinary women, too. Yet their life mattered to God, and they made a difference.

Where did they get the courage to leave their lives behind and follow thirteen men around the arid countryside for three years? Maybe you don't want to leave your prison-like life behind because it means leaving something you are comfortable with—even if it sucks and even if it hurts, at least you know how to navigate it, right? But here's the thing: You were never meant to live a small life. If you really want to leave your small life behind, you have to want to change. These women changed radically.

This tribe of traveling women had quite a few "Marys" in it: Mary, Jesus' mother; Mary, the mother of James and Joses; and Mary Magdalene. Along with these Marys, several other women traveled with them as well: Salome (who turned out to be Jesus' aunt), Susanna, and Joanna. Many other women followed along as well, but these specific women named in scripture financially cared for Jesus and His twelve disciples. They supported them while they made their way through the Judean countryside to Jerusalem, where Jesus would eventually hang on a wooden cross upon a hill called Golgotha.

During this time in the world, women weren't educated, they didn't pursue careers, and they didn't have many choices to do something different with their lives. They rarely had their own money, and they were shamed if they didn't fit in with the culture by getting married and having children. (They were especially shamed for not bearing children.) Their voices weren't heard in the community, in the temple, or by the men they knew. Women were basically ignored.

However, Jesus didn't ignore the women. Instead, He expressed their importance and value by including them in His ministry. Each woman was significant to God's plan in Israel in those times, but she had to give up something to answer the call on her life. I think she did this because, after encountering Jesus, she wanted nothing more than to follow Him wherever He went, doing whatever she could to support His work on earth.

It is very likely that these traveling women left behind spouses, children, homes, friends and the available income of their husbands. Some of them left behind a powerful position in their community like Joanna who was the wife of the man who ran King Herod's household —she was rubbing shoulders with royalty.

They left behind their own bed and kitchen table. They were the ones who ran ahead to the next town, setting up a makeshift camp for a band of men who were a day behind them hungry and tired. God's plan for these women was to financially support Jesus while He made His way to Golgotha. Their funds provided for everyone—but how? The Bible doesn't tell us where they got the funds, but as with all of God's plans and ways, He provided what was needed. He equipped these women with the financial means to support His Son's mission. It is another one of God's mysteries.

I AM THE LIGHT

You might be thinking, *Oh, those poor women! To give up everything they had or knew to follow Jesus around the desert, to give up their kids and husbands—count me out!* But I don't think it was like that. I believe they wanted to do the work they were called to do because they had encountered Jesus in their life. They wanted to be near Him and hear

His kind words. They wanted to witness His power, see the miracles He performed, and watch the people get healed. They wanted to feel His love showered down upon them and be adored by Him.

He didn't ignore them. He listened to them. He loved their uniqueness and their quirky ways. He showed each woman she was valuable, and she mattered to God. He illuminated their hearts with Himself. I know this because this is who He is, and this is how He treats me, as well.

Jesus said, *"I am the light of the world. If you follow me, you won't have to walk in darkness, because you will have the light that leads to life"* (John 8:12, NLT). This rips my heart wide open. I want to follow Him, too, wherever He is taking me.

BEGINNING TO SEE THE LIGHT

I eventually climbed out of the bleak basement, landed a new job, and moved into a small condo in a bedroom community outside the city limits. All God's plan, no doubt.

A friend asked me to go to a new-age seminar on how to get happy and discover my purpose in life. This wasn't a bad idea because everything I had been doing so far was an act of hatred towards myself. And I was beginning to wonder why in the world was I in this world. I needed a purpose. Why was I even here? I wanted to be significant in a world of insignificance and to make a difference somehow. I'd been torturing myself for thirty-five years, trying to fill up that empty, black hole with stuff. There had to be another way to live because what I'd been doing so far wasn't working.

I met Steve at that weekend seminar. The Saturday afternoon assignment was to grab a partner and talk about your worst relationship over the lunch break. Oh, brother. To a woman who doesn't talk about herself, this was a problem. I'd learned early in life to shut up and not say a word.

You can imagine how the luncheon went. We talked about our exes, and he sounded like he'd gotten it all together. He and his ex were even really good friends, whereas I didn't want to see mine ever again (let alone iron out issues and be friends).

For most of the other assignments during the weekend when we needed a partner, Steve and I drifted together. At the end of the weekend for the Sunday evening event, we stood in a circle and passed a candle around, giving thanks or some such thing. When I passed the candle to Steve, I said something I would never say to a guy —especially a gorgeous one like him: "I would love to have you in my life for the rest of my life, even if it's as a friend." I looked around behind me, wondering who in the world just said that. I hadn't thought of saying those words, so why did they slip out of my mouth so easily?

He did the double-take, and then our circle broke up. We were separated, the evening was over, and I went home. He called me the next day and asked me out on a date for Friday night. We went out for sushi and afterwards for a drive along the ocean.

I have to admit I just about bailed on the date. He was way too nice, and I was used to the bad guys in the room. This man was different; his eyes welled up with tears when he spoke about his ex-wife. This was someone beautiful, a man with a heart.

Who had put those words into my mouth? God?

We eventually married and began living a good life together. A house, a little puppy dog, friends, fine neighbours, steady paycheques. Did I love myself? I was getting better at it. Did I have a sense of significance like I mattered to anyone? I felt significant to him—that was a start.

How did I cope with struggles and hopelessness? I began walking a happier path on most days. Was I still seeking approval from everyone? Yes, still trying to be perfect and fit in. I tried to fit into the corporate world, climbing a ladder I really wasn't interested in, seeking significance there and a sense of purpose. Did it work? Not really, I was successful, earned a bonus every year but still struggled to fit in. This didn't seem like a good enough reason as to why I was born either.

THE BLUE BIBLE

One day, I found a small, blue Bible in our bookshelf. It wasn't mine. When I asked Steve if it was his, he said it must have been in his mom's belongings he got when she passed away. Hmmm. It was a small little book with tiny letters and Jesus' words were in red ink, the colour of Jesus' blood, and the language was old-fashioned—stiff and awkward. I'd find out later it was a King James Version of The Bible.

Steve had gone away for the weekend, traveling for work, so I was on my own which was okay—I do alone quite well. I sprawled out on the carpet in the middle of the living room with a cup of tea to read this little book, and honestly, I couldn't put it down. I read away the weekend, not really knowing what I was reading. It was a story I had never heard or read before.

After I read most of the blue Bible, an idea was planted in my heart to check out a church. We lived across the street from one, so I would secretly watch the activity on Sunday mornings, and I can tell you this much: I didn't want to be one of those Christian women dressed up in those boring church clothes (the Liz Claiborne navy-blue blazer look) looking like they never had bad breath or smelly armpits.

So, I was in a quandary. You see, I'd sworn off going to church at seven, but now I was being mysteriously guided to go. I didn't like what was walking in and out of the church across the street—I didn't look like those women and I didn't want to.

One evening, an acquaintance of ours mentioned a church about three miles away from our house where she had gone a few times, and it was apparently "come as you are." They would take anybody in, so this sounded like the place I could take the risk of slipping in and out of without getting noticed too much—just checking it out. Another piece of the puzzle is that a client of mine happened to go to this church and was a friend to this acquaintance—they both worked for the same company. Coincidence?

MY FIRST DAY AT CHURCH

Steve agreed to go along with me to church that Sunday. I had no experience of church and was full of questions: what to wear, what to say, how to act. Is it okay to wear makeup? What should I say? I decided to wear a dress like I was going to a cocktail party—better to dress up than down to a cocktail party—so I thought this was a good place to start.

I was quite nervous and shook in the car all the way to the church. You'd think I was going to be asked to get up on the pulpit to say a few words, introduce myself to the congregation, and tell them all the bad things I'd been doing since I was last there. None of this happened. Instead, we walked into the foyer of the church, and there was my client and his wife with a baby daughter slung on her hip. A friendly face. We chatted for a few minutes and then followed the music beginning to play in the main part of the church.

I felt a sense of calmness and peace begin to seep in. Maybe it was because there was a familiar face to greet us, but I don't think so because when we started to sing the songs, a funny thing happened: It felt like I had been singing those songs of praise for my whole life.

It was peaceful being there—my anxiety slipped away. This is the church where I became a follower of Jesus and was baptized a few years later. This is the church I was sitting in when I received a clear message from God to write for him and where this book became a seed planted in my heart.

God works in wonderful, beautiful, and mysterious ways. The pastor at this church was on fire! Pastor Brian Buhler preached powerfully and passionately, asking, "Have you asked Jesus into your heart?" This was just like the last time I was in church at age seven. You'd think this would've killed it for me, but it didn't—not this time. It felt like he was looking right into my eyes and preaching directly to me and only to me. How did he know the exact words, message, and story to illuminate for me on that Sunday? Surely Pastor Brian didn't...but God did.

How did God know I wouldn't run away this time? Lovingly, He knows the best way to illuminate the path of each one of His broken-down children. He knows exactly who to put in our path, too. Oh, this makes it easy then, doesn't it? He does the planning and the work, and I simply say yes.

What I needed then more than anything was a powerful, righteous, but friendly voice and a message that went along with it to help me make sense of the madness in our world. I was hungry for the truth. Not *a* truth, not *somebody else's* truth but *The* Truth. At this church, I discovered there was a different way to live, and there was one truth, one God, and one way to come close to Him.

I didn't become a follower of Jesus that Sunday. It took me months to take the risk and invite Him to come into my heart and life. Jesus knew this, so He waited and made me even hungrier for Him. He illuminated the path through words, songs, messages, and people, and every Sunday it seemed as though Pastor Brian was preaching just for me. He was one of the most powerful pastors and gifted speakers I've heard, bringing us passionate messages of hope and truth of Jesus each week. Now I look back and see just how much Jesus loves me— He created this convoluted web of people and circumstances which eventually put me on a pilgrimage to Him.

My client's wife, Tina, became one of my dearest sisters and was instrumental in me opening my heart wide to Jesus. She wasn't dressed in the standard navy-blue blazer like I thought all Christian women wore. Instead, she had a strong Bohemian look going, and that was comforting to me. I know this may sound funny to some, but I am serious. Her appearance, honesty, and loveliness actually helped to blow apart my own preconceived idea of "Christian women," and I began to feel I just might fit in.

SAYING YES

I invited Jesus into my heart twice. Why twice? Because I was a perfectionist and a people-pleaser, so I did things twice to make sure I got it right. *He probably didn't hear me the first time.* Does this sound familiar to you?

I invited Him in while sitting quietly in the church and then again publicly at a retreat called "The Alpha Program." We were in break-out sessions when I prayed aloud a prayer to invite Jesus into my heart and life. A few women took me aside and prayed over me while I wept. Another beautiful thing happened: When I cried during this time, it didn't hurt.

During all my weeping in the past, it hurt. I mean it really hurt. My throat was usually so tied up in knots I could barely breathe, and it stung as if razor blades were moving up and down my esophagus. This time, I wept with ease. It felt like a ton of steel had been lifted out of me, and all the hurt—the knots and the rusted mess—flew away into the atmosphere as peace fell upon me. It didn't hurt to cry. Instead, I wept tears—which I can only describe as joyful tears. This was something I had never experienced.

I lived a lifetime of making bad choices. I see this now, but it took a solid forty years of wandering around the back country with a huge yoke of shame, guilt, and insecurity on my shoulders and a heart full of tied knots from feeling unloved and rejected before I made any kind of a choice towards God. But I did make a choice. I finally said yes.

He came for me in the only way it would work for me. He perfectly illuminates the path to Himself for each one of His kids who really and truly want to get to know Him. Why not a burning bush for me? Why not a life altering conversion for me? Why not a near death experience? I didn't have any of these experiences (not that I wanted any one of them) but whatever it is that He did to me, all I know is today I want more of God.

It seems He performed some sort of a miracle on me, knowing where I came from and who I swore off so long ago. He pursues each one of us uniquely because He knows every hair on our head. He knows us intrinsically, and He knows the words we speak even before they are thoughts in our minds. It is no surprise to God where I am in my pilgrimage to Him at any moment in any given day.

> *"You see me when I travel and when I rest at home. You know everything I do. You know what I am going to say even before I say it, Lord."*
>
> — PSALM 139:3-4, NLT

I became His daughter the minute I invited Him in, but please, let me be crystal clear here: It has taken years and years for me to live like His daughter. In the hidden places of my heart, I needed and still need to invite Him in and ask Him to heal and untie some more knots. I still hunger to live a better story, and I still hunger for more of God.

THE ILLUMINATING GOD

The Illuminating God shines His brilliant love into our hearts. This is how it was meant to be all along—our hearts connected to God's so we would shine every minute of every day in His love. We were never meant to be separated from God, but tragically we are. We are all disconnected in our spirits until we invite Jesus to reconnect us back to God.

He does this differently for everyone. Some He pulls slowly with gradual baby steps, like me. Some He impacts with lighting and thunder and some with a soft tender glow. This is how wonderfully personal and loving He is. God wants us to learn about Him, read about Him, and gather more information, but He mostly wants us to experience Him. He is with us through the Holy Spirit whom Jesus sent.

WHO IS THIS HOLY SPIRIT ANYWAY?

When I first became a believer, this Holy Spirit person was really hard to comprehend. I could understand God as Father and Creator of everything. I could understand Jesus as The Son of God who came to earth to save me. But the Holy Spirit seemed like this elusive, spiritual type, floating around, blowing this way and that way like the wind. It was hard for me to grasp who He was and what He did.

Pastor Brian explained the Holy Spirit so clearly one day in a sermon which I have never forgotten. He explained that the Holy Spirit is the experiential Person of God—the way we experience God on earth. Okay, that made sense. When my eyes well up with tears while reading a verse in Scripture, this is the Holy Spirit. When my heart led me unwaveringly one day to venture down into the eastside of town and encounter a woman there, this was the Holy Spirit. When my heart pounded in church one day to get baptized and to write this book, this was the Holy Spirit.

The Holy Spirit's purpose is to prepare us to meet Jesus, and then, when we invite Jesus into our heart and life, He helps us be more like Jesus. He also guides us into the truth of who God is, and besides all this, He does something wonderful—*He comforts us.* I know this may seem confusing, but don't fret about this because the Holy Spirit will help you to understand everything about God—it's His job. And He will explain it better and more personally than I can.

A NEW CREATION

Our Father wants a relationship with us, so He will do everything in His supernatural power to get us into one. Like the traveling women, our part is to say *yes*, to believe, and then to walk the way He illuminates for us. If we fall down, it's no big deal—He's still there for us, and He will light up the way for us over and over and over again. He will do this forever until the very end. It's His promise to us.

When your spirit is illuminated by Jesus, there is no turning back, so if you want to change your life and your heart—I mean really want to change—He will do it! He'll come in and transform your life. He did this for me. I didn't stay the way I was—always taking, sinning, devouring, creating chaos, lacking gratitude, living under the shadow of shame and guilt, never feeling worthy to be loved, and never feeling good enough.

Now, everything in my life is different because I am His. I can wear the crown that says I am loved, I am significant, I am adored, and I matter. I am His daughter princess, crowned with an inheritance into eternity, and you too can be His precious daughter. And not only will He illuminate your heart and spirit, He will light up the way for you to walk.

This is why I want to go to church, read The Bible, praise Him with singing and dancing, and offer my money to his church. I want to drive through rain and snow to hook up with friends who are on the same spiritual walk as I am. I want to do these things because of love, not fear.

Do you know what happens when you believe in Him, invite Him into your heart and life, and let Him be your King? The Spirit of God touches the place deep inside of you set aside for Him and this place—your spirit—comes alive. This is why believers dance and sing about Jesus living in us because He truly does! Our spirits, hearts, and minds become brand new, and so He says we are a new creation.[1]

TRULY ILLUMINATING

Illumination is letting His light into our heart. A heart lit with God's love lights up the rest of our life. How do we let the light come into those dark knotted places within us? Jesus will do the work and illuminate a good way for us to walk. God doesn't want to merely change our circumstances, our careers, or our marital status (although He can do this, too); God wants to change us. He wants to change the very essence of us—our hearts. And He will...if we will let Him.

> *"And this hope is not a disappointing fantasy, because we can now experience the endless love of God cascading into our hearts through the Holy Spirit who lives in us!"*
>
> *— ROMANS 5:5, TPT*

PRAY

Here is a small prayer you can say out loud or in your heart—either way He will hear you:

> *Oh, Jesus. I am so tired of living the way I have been living. I want to leave my old ways behind and start fresh. Forgive me for all the mistakes I've made, I am sorry they happened. Please shine Your light into my heart, and show me a better way. I am ready to change my life and I am asking for your help. Please help me. Amen.*

SOMETHING TO PONDER

Do you ever wonder why you are here? Have you ever wondered what your purpose is? Are you tired of feeling you are insignificant and don't matter? Are you curious at all about the real truth of this chaotic world we live in?

> *"Show me your ways, Lord, teach me your paths. Guide me in your truth and teach me, for you are God my Savior, and my hope is in you all day long."*
>
> *— PSALM 25:4-5, NIV*

THE SPILLING GOD AND A SINFUL WOMAN

"Your love is like a flooding river
overflowing its banks with kindness."
— Psalm 103:8, TPT —

"As long as there is a God in heaven, there is grace on earth,
and I am the spilling God of the uncontainable,
forever-overflowing-love-grace."[1]
— Ann Voskamp —

od spills His love and grace all over us. Daughters, sisters, moms, aunts, baby girls, and grandmothers. He covers us with it if we let Him.

WHAT IS GRACE THEN?

Grace is God's loving-kindness and favour. Grace doesn't come from the world, our dog-eat-dog world. In this culture, we compete and work for everything we get. We are trained from childhood to do so. If you eat your dinner, you'll get dessert. If you get straight A's on your report card, you'll get into university. If you get a good paying job, you can buy a house, boat, designer clothes. If you make your sales quota, you'll keep your job, and if you don't, you won't.

The world says anything good we receive we have to earn. If we don't earn it, we don't deserve it. Grace is the complete opposite: We get gifts of love and favour and we never even have to work for it. We don't strive for the gift, we get it freely. This is Jesus.

THE GIFT LADY

There was a lady who lived down the hill from us when I was growing up who reminds me of grace. "Grace" should have been her name. She had a chubby cocker spaniel who barked his head off when I walked by, so she would come out of the kitchen door and ask the little fella to be quiet. Then she would call out my name and ask me to come over to the fence, which I did. She would disappear into the house and come back out with a gift. It was usually something small and adorable, maybe a hair ribbon or a cookie.

One day, she had something for me that was extraordinary. It was an exquisite doll standing on a pedestal about ten inches high. The doll's dress was made out of a peach coloured foam fabric cut as delicate autumn leaves with a tiny pearl set into the middle of each leaf. Her bonnet matched the dress perfectly. She was the most glorious doll I had ever seen. *And it was for me.*

I had never received such a wonderful gift, and I didn't have to do anything to get it. I was only walking by and trying to avoid her yappy dog. When I think of this lady giving such a beautiful gift to a poor girl who lived up the hill, I think of God's grace—freely given with no strings attached.

His blood spilled out on the ground at a place called Golgotha so everyone could be set straight with God. Everyone? Yes, and even if every person on earth wants His love and grace, He has enough to go around. The river of God has plenty of water.[2] He came to spill out His grace and fill you with His love. He came to save you and make you His own daughter for all eternity. He came to offer you a different life. If He could change my self-absorbed soul and heart and set me on a better path, He can do the same for you.

GRACE CONQUERS SHAME

"Shame is a negative and disturbing emotional experience involving feelings of self-condemnation and the desire to hide the damaged self from others (Lewis, 1992; Tangney, 1995). It is a state in which the whole self feels defective, often as a result of a perceived failure to meet social and self-imposed standards."[3]

— CANDICE FEIRING AND LYNN S. TASKA

Shame is actually much worse than this technical description—shame is a destroyer of life. Shame rips out our heart and puts a hard knot in its place. It steals our identity and takes away the love we were meant to receive and give. Shame eats away at our soul. It creates a chaotic mind and a negative attitude. No longer are we confident women after receiving and being shamed; we are women in prison, surrounded by walls too hard to break through on our own.

We can't dream. We can't fly. We can't express beauty. We can't sing, dance, or love ourselves, and we can't claim the big beautiful life we were meant to have. Shame is our captor and enemy. How are we ever going to get away from this captor? The only way I know of is through Jesus.

He came to give me freedom from my shame along with everything else I felt guilty and condemned about. He did this with an abundance of love and grace. A breathtaking amount.

Grace spilled into our world for everyone when Jesus hung on the cross and bled there until he died. He did this for me and you. Instead of me paying for all the messes, wrong-doings, and stupid things I've done all my life, He took the punishment. He paid for all my messes, and now, in the eyes of God, I am free from them. Not only that, but Jesus stands in front of Father God for me and says: "She's good. Your daughter is good." What does the Father do? He looks at Jesus, His beautiful Son, and He says that He doesn't remember any of the terrible, nasty things I've ever done. This is His promise to us:

> *"...as far as the east is from the west, so far has he removed our transgressions from us."*
>
> — PSALM 103:12, NIV

This is grace.

> *Thank you, Lord, for Your grace which I don't fully understand the workings of—but thank You anyway for giving it to me. Thank You for grabbing me out of chaos, setting me on a path for eternity, blasting me with love, giving me hope and a purpose, and then pouring Your grace out all over my life. What would I be without You, The Spilling God, coming into my life and healing me? I would still be the walking dead.*

A SINFUL WOMAN

A sinful woman took a risk. She bought an alabaster jar of perfume which cost her a small fortune and walked over to Simon's home with it, where a dinner party was taking place. Jesus was in the house, and there was no way He was leaving town without her getting in to see Him. She wanted to bless Him with her perfume.

Somehow, she managed to get inside the house; maybe a servant let her in, or the kitchen door was ajar, and she was able to slip through it. It doesn't matter—she got in. She saw where Jesus was reclining at a table and quietly positioned herself behind Him. But something happened she hadn't expected. She was emotionally moved being in His atmosphere, and she began to weep.

She is described as an immoral woman, a social outcast and not esteemed in the village she lived in because of her lifestyle. I always wonder why she was there that day to bless and give thanks. Why did she buy an expensive jar of perfume and intentionally go to a dinner party she wasn't invited to? Surely something really big had happened in her life to warrant the risk she was taking. Think about it.

The alabaster jar of perfume was extreme—a year's wages, maybe more. When we thank someone who does something special for us, we drop off a box of chocolates and a card on their doorstep or send flowers with a $50 price tag...not a year's wages. Whoever gives thanks on a grand scale like this woman must have had her life transformed in an extraordinary way. Did Jesus drive demons out of her and restore her life?

She kneels in front of Jesus crying, her tears spill onto His feet, and then she does something even more intimate and unexpected—she wipes her tears away with her hair and then gently kisses His feet. She picks up her alabaster jar and pours the perfume all over His feet.

The host was miffed, and the guests were not impressed with what they had just witnessed. *Is this guy really a prophet? I doubt it, or he wouldn't be letting this woman touch him. What a joke? How'd she get in here anyways?*

Jesus knew exactly what they were thinking and hit them square in the face with a question. I love it when He does this.

> *"So, let me ask you this Simon. There are two people who owe money to a lender, one owes a lot and the other owes a little, but they both can't repay the money so, out of kindness, the lender agrees to forgive the debt of both people. Who do you think will feel the most forgiveness and will actually love the lender the most?"*

> — LUKE 7:41-42, NIV

This is obvious, isn't it? The person who owed $100,000 is going to love the lender much more than the person who owed $1,000.

She was still kneeling at Jesus' feet, wiping the perfume and tears with her hair while He continued to speak with Simon. He compared the actions of Simon towards Him at the dinner party with her actions of the tears, hair, and perfume. It was extravagant, and the comparison was extreme. Simon wasn't as grateful, welcoming, or kind as he could have been, and there is a big reason why he should have been oozing with thanksgiving. Jesus had just healed him of leprosy. Why wasn't he more grateful? This is the story of mankind.

Jesus told them all that someone who has been forgiven for a large amount of sin in their life will love God far more passionately than someone who had little to be forgiven of.[4]

Then Jesus looked at the woman with love in His heart, and in front of everyone at the dinner party, He said three beautiful truths to her: Her sins are forgiven, she has a new life, and she can now walk in peace.[5]

By acknowledging her gift, He accepted her. He didn't push her away when she came up behind Him with the perfume, and He didn't say, *You don't belong here and you're not good enough.* He didn't stop her from weeping or tell her, *You're just too much.* Instead He accepted her in front of everyone who was there—which means eventually everyone in her own hometown who had rejected and ignored her. He wasn't looking at the mess she had been dragging around all her life but instead at the beauty hidden within her heart.

Hopefully, you are encouraged by this story. This is one of my most treasured stories in Scripture, affirming to me how important we are to God and to His divine plan. He desperately wants to give us a crown to wear. But He isn't going to force you to do anything. He will be available to you, He will fight for you, He will chase after you, He will bust you out of prison and will rescue you, He will be unstoppable in His pursuit of you, and He will catch you when you finally decide to say yes...but not until then.

FREEDOM TO SAY YES

God gave us a gift called free will, which means we can do whatever we want. But it's been God's plan all along that you would actually choose Him and His ways in the free will gift He has given you. Imagine free will at its best: You are free to love, free to express, free to create, free to fly, free to sing and dance, and so on. Unfortunately, free will also gives you freedom to drink yourself into a stupor every day, to gamble away your rent money every month, or to eat as much food as you can to stuff your emotions down. Whatever you think you have freedom in could actually be what owns you. You might want to think about this some more. The thing you think you have freedom in is what owns you.

Why do I say this? I say it from experience. The thing I thought I had freedom in—living the way I wanted without God—was the thing which ruled my life with terrible results. I lived a life without God and missed out on His love and grace for forty years, and instead of loving myself, I disliked myself quite a bit. I don't want you to live this way, and I have written this book in the hope you will accept God's love and grace and live the life you were meant to live.

> *"You intended to harm me, but God intended it all for good."*
>
> — GENESIS 50:20A, NIV

PAYING FOR MY SINS?

Before I became a follower of Jesus, I didn't think about sin, Christ Jesus, or anybody paying for any of my mistakes. I didn't think about God at all. Heck, I didn't even know I was really doing anything wrong let alone "sinning." I never thought I would eventually be expected to pay up. I didn't know I needed saving. Saving from what?

I lived my life from paycheque to paycheque, hangover to hangover, heartache to heartache, and depression to depression. I lived like millions of women do who live without the knowledge that they need to be saved. I am serious about this. When I finally became aware of Jesus and the truth about the spiritual world, it became clear how dangerously I had been living. (And I was sick of it by then anyway.) I came to the staggering realization that I was going to have to face the consequences.

But I didn't want to pay for the consequences of all the terrible things I had done, especially the things I'd done to my loved ones and even to myself. What good news it was to my battered and fearful heart to find out that Jesus paid God the price on my behalf. This is the supernatural grace of The Spilling God.

FACING THE CONSEQUENCES

I don't want to give you the impression, though, that you can go about doing a bunch of terrible things and not pay any consequences just because you're covered by God's grace. There will always be consequences for our actions, good or bad, whether we believe in Jesus or not. The ancient Biblical truth of reaping what you sow is steadfast. As a believer, I can get trapped in sin and will suffer the consequences of those actions, but here is the beauty of Jesus: I don't have to live feeling guilty or ugly because of what I've done. And I don't have to earn my way back to being in His good books. I simply need to ask for forgiveness one more time, and His grace spills out for me.

> *"The Lord is close to all whose hearts are crushed by pain, and he is always ready to restore the repentant one."*

> — PSALM 34:18, TPT

Once God has spilled His grace into our life and forgiven us, there are a few things we need to do in order to continue in His ways: forgive others and forgive ourselves.

FORGIVING OTHERS

One of my favourite Lyle Lovett songs sums up our stubbornness to forgive others. The line goes something like this: The difference between me and God—he'll forgive you but I won't, he'll forgive you but I don't. Lyle was singing about his lover who has cheated on him again and how he was not able or even willing to forgive her. This is the human heart. We can't do anything on our own no matter how much we think we can. No human heart is like the heart of God, but with Jesus, we can get closer and closer.

> *"Move your heart closer and closer to God, and he will come even closer to you."*
>
> — JAMES 4:8, TPT

Forgiving those who have hurt us is hard to do, but we need to do it if we want to live a better story. This doesn't mean we forget what has happened to us. In my experience, forgiveness meant that the hurt I carried around in my heart began to fade away. I had to forgive the old man who molested me. I had to forgive my ex-husband, and I also had to forgive my mom.

We have to forgive, or at least cry out the words and mean them, and God will do the rest. It's a mystery how God's forgiveness works, but it does.

FORGIVING OURSELVES

I don't want to live the rest of my life hating myself for all the mistakes I've made in my life. God sees me so separated from those mistakes. Why does He do this? I can think of one reason only: He has compassion for all He has made—that includes you and me, His favoured women.

I know how hard my heart can be at times, and I know the messy things I'm capable of doing, so to forgive myself is a tough one. Thankfully, God knows my heart, too, and He still forgives me. If God forgives me, but I haven't forgiven myself yet, this means I think I don't deserve it. This is a lie, of course. If you think the same thing, I encourage you to fight to believe the opposite.

It is essential to allow God's forgiveness to spill into your life and for you to receive it. Then you can love and forgive yourself as best you can. This is how the shame I carried around inside my soul was conquered—by His love and grace. Shame no longer has its tight grip on me. We ask for forgiveness, and He is pleased to do it. Our part is to believe and trust He has forgiven us. Then we must forgive ourselves because God has.

This forgiveness business might sound too easy. It doesn't make logical sense, and some of us want to know how it all works. I can't answer that question for you because I don't know how God works. He just does. I don't know how gravity works, but I know it does.

"As you do not know the path of the wind, or how the body is formed in a mother's womb, so you cannot understand the work of God, the Maker of all things."

— ECCLESIASTES 11:5, NIV

God gave me a beautiful vision one night while writing this book. I saw myself gathering up my teeter-tottering three-year-old self into my own loving arms, holding her, and rocking her quietly. Then God showed me a vision of Himself picking up that same heart-broken little girl into His arms while His love light was spilling out all over me. I sat on His lap, and He drew my head close to His chest while He said, *"It's okay. I've got you My child. You can come back to this place anytime. Anytime. I've got you."*

He is the unseen God, so nobody knows what He looks like, but the presence of God in my vision was a billowing white spirit of arms and wings enveloping me. I've waited my whole life to have a Father wrap His arms around me. I know God loves me, and I know I am His daughter. He's got me. He will do this for you.

THE SPILLING GOD

The Spilling God poured grace on the sinful woman at the dinner party and transformed her life of unacceptance, feeling unwanted, and unloved into a life of forgiveness, freedom, and peace. She became one of His daughters, and He placed the gift of a crown of His peace, salvation, and acceptance upon her lovely head, and she didn't even have to earn it. Oh, this is my story, too!

You may think you don't need God's saving grace at all. The beautiful sun is shining in your world and life seems to be all sunshine and lollipops today. Your kids are actually listening to you. Your husband really loves you. Your house is perfect. Your career is humming along, and your bank account is flush. Everything in your life and world seems perfect.

Yet, there lingers an emptiness. A bit of sadness or melancholy creeps in and leaves you unhappy or depressed one more time. Perhaps you do need God's very own fingers to pry apart the bloodied strings in your heart and set you free from your pain.

TRULY SPILLING

The Spilling God will pour out all the grace, love, and forgiveness your heart needs. He will open it up to let all the love flow out. He is the best-ever solution for your broken heart and soul. Give your brokenness to Him, and let Him carry it.

He did the work for you already. He took all the punishment for the things you've done wrong. Everything you've ever done, which you secretly knew someday you were going to have to pay for, He will take it from you and kill it at the cross. Your part is to believe and receive this miracle of grace that He is offering you. You can choose to live with Him at the center of your life...as best you can...every day.

And when you seem to mess up again, Jesus will take you back right then and there. No questions asked. No wagging of a finger in front of your face. No "I told you so" or "You should be ashamed of yourself." Instead He says, *"All your sins are forgiven"* (Luke 7:48, TPT). This is the love and grace of the Spilling God.

God will give each woman His spilling love and overflowing, never-ending grace simply by her asking.

PRAY

You don't have to pray these exact words, but this might prompt you. I encourage you to say whatever is in your heart, and He will answer you.

> *Jesus, please forgive me for all the wrong things I've done in my life. I don't deserve to be forgiven for them, but You have promised if I ask, I will be forgiven. So, I'm asking. Help me to live a better story, free from all this guilt-ridden anxiety, and please unburden my heart from this heaviness. I'm tired of feeling guilty for everything I've done, and I want a new, fresh way. Amen.*

If there are specific things you want forgiveness for, let Him know what they are. He knows them already, but sometimes to speak and name them loosens their power over us. This is another mystery of God.

SOMETHING TO PONDER

Examine your life, and ask yourself if there is something that you think you have freedom in but it actually owns you. Do you believe you need saving at all, or do you believe that it's for somebody else and not you? Do you need to forgive somebody? Do you need to forgive yourself? Perhaps you do need God to breathe His beautiful divine Spirit into you after all.

A few poetic words to bless you:

His blood spilling out at the foot of the cross
to my outstretched hands below.
When His blood finally touches me,
I'm as clean as fallen snow.

THE SINGING GOD AND THE FIRST DAUGHTER

"The LORD your God is with you, he is mighty to save. He will take great delight in you, he will quiet you with his love, he will rejoice over you with singing."
— Zephaniah 3:17, NIV —

Who sings over you?

Our mothers used to sing over us with nursery rhymes and lullabies, rocking us to sleep every night, but after a season of lullabies is over, there's a pretty slim chance anybody is going to be singing over us.

Maybe you believe you aren't worthy enough or loveable enough for anybody to delight in you so much that they would actually sing over you. I am convinced you are exactly this loveable and worthy. Open your heart and mind to the idea that there is a Singing God who bends down over you from Heaven—*from Heaven*, imagine that! He brings peace to your hectic mind and empty, sad heart.

God whispers this message to me for you, dear reader:

Let them know I bring peace to My daughters.

My soul used to be so empty it felt like a black hole inside of me, and my heart was crammed full of protective knots: Knots of lost worth, abandonment, and rejection. Knots of hurting words, knots of "You couldn't," "You'll never be," and "You should be ashamed of yourself." Maybe you have knots in your heart, too, ready to be loosened. Maybe yours have been tied even tighter while trying to find a way to fix yourself. Maybe you tried a self-help program that encouraged learning to walk on hot coals—what a loser if you can't master this feat! Or, perhaps you tried the self-help books that want you to forget all about God and just do it your way—you are "god" after all, so you are the power! Maybe you listened obediently to motivational speakers urging you to get your peace and power from your "goddess-within" or your "internal wolf-woman."

Fix myself? Really? But I'm the one who got me in this mess in the first place, and I thought I was doing a great job trying to fix my goddess, wolf-woman thingy. You see how complicated it can be. I've read all the books and done all of these things. (Okay, I admit I never walked on a bed of hot coals, but you get my drift.) They work for the moment, but then my feet start to cool down, and I'm not so "hot on myself" anymore. This was usually when I would start cramming stuff into my empty soul again. I want to get the knots untied and keep them untied, and I want this dark emptiness to go away. Jesus says it's impossible for me to do this kind of heart work, I need Him to do it for me.

Here's why Jesus has to do it for us. There is an empty dark place inside all of us, an emptiness we try to snuff out or fill up. We try to stuff it full of booze, food, drugs, or seventy-five pairs of shoes.

That place nags at us every day if we don't attend to it. It is the place where the aching is unbearable at times, and it appears as if nothing will fill it up completely, once and for all. However, instead of changing our lives by following Jesus and letting Him do the work, we play around with other things we think can make us whole... How about a new car? A designer coat? A vodka bottle hidden in your desk at work?

Does working eighteen hours a day help you feel better about yourself? What about busyness? If we are busy, busy, busy every day, then we really don't have to think about the emptiness lurking around inside of us. This sad cycle won't just end on its own.

I want to share a way to fill up the emptiness you have been experiencing all these years. First, though, I want to let you know what the emptiness is. It's the spirit God placed in you—the spot, or secret place, where God wants to connect with you. But it's dead for the moment; it's not been ignited or brought to life yet, and this is why we have such a longing and a desire to fill this part of us up.

You and I were born spiritually dead—we all were. You may be thinking that with your own power you can bring the empty, black hole to life. Or perhaps you think that if you cram it up with a bunch of stuff, it will simply go away—the emptiness and longing along with it. The longing is for God and from God though, so that's not going to work. The only way to get rid of this black hole is to let God do it for you. This place needs filling by God and only God because He created your spirit as a place to meet with you.

It's a mystery and a miracle, and as I've mentioned a few times, we aren't meant to know everything. Mysteriously, He keeps the longing in our hearts going for Him because only through Him can our dead spirit be brought to life. He is waiting for you to ask Him to ignite your spirit. When this happens, you become God's child, and He becomes your Father. This is the reason Jesus Christ came to earth— it's His job to bring you back home to be with Father God for eternity.

This is the truth of Jesus Christ. This is what I know to be true for myself and others who believe in Christ, and so I want to share it with you so you too can be with your Father in eternity. I hope the alternative of not being with God is never an option for you.

We all have an amazing, divine life planned out for us by God. He has breathed into us these beautiful gifts which are meant to be breathed back out to others. If they aren't breathed back out because of our hard heart, then what happens? Do the gifts diminish? They may diminish completely, lost forever, unless we can open our hearts wide so the love-gifts begin to flow like a living, divine stream out of us onto others.

My knots were untied with one encouraging word from God at a time, one act of love and grace at a time, and one beautiful encounter with Him at a time. This is what God does—He unties the knots in our hearts and lets the love, forgiveness, grace, and our individual giftings flow back out to others.

FROM THE BEGINNING

"He has made everything beautiful in its time."

— ECCLESIASTES 3:11, NIV

Have you heard the story of Adam and Eve? It seems impossible to connect all the dots and understand our broken relationship with God unless we look back to the garden of Eden to see what happened there.

Here is my plain and simple version. In the beginning God created everything, and on the sixth day He made a man and a woman. He was so overjoyed with them that He said they were very good.[1] Both were created equally by God and placed in the most fabulous place ever—a beautiful and lush garden.

It was joyous in the Garden of Eden because God was there. Adam and Eve walked around chit-chatting with God every day. Can you imagine hanging out with God in a perfect garden? I can't wait.

They weren't just hanging out in the garden, God gave them something to do. He asked them to tend the garden. I think this is why people love to garden so much. It is the fundamental work God gave to the first people He created.

It seems everything was perfect until the devil came along and started pestering Eve about trees and fruit and... "Really, God said that? He doesn't want you to touch what? Doesn't want you to know what He knows? Phfft. Go ahead, give it a try and then you'll be just like God."[2] Those lies were flying out of his mouth, and she gave in to them.

Eve decided to take a bite from the fruit of the Tree of the Knowledge of Good and Evil. Let me clarify about that tree: It wasn't the tree of knowledge—it was the Tree of the Knowledge of Good and Evil. Before the bite of forbidden fruit, Adam and Eve had no knowledge of evil. Period. But the bite changed everything.

Immediately, things changed in the garden, just like God said it would "...you must not eat from the tree of the knowledge of good and evil, for when you eat of it you will surely die."[3] Instantly, (not eventually but instantly) their spiritual connection with God changed from being alive to being dead. Now, Adam and Eve knew all about evil and death.

When God found the two of them hiding behind a bush naked in their shame, He did the most loving thing He could have done: He banned them from the garden. Why was this loving? I used to think this was the cruelest thing God could have done, but it wasn't because in the middle of the garden there was also the tree of life. If either of them would have then eaten from the tree of life, they would have lived for all eternity in the state of "good and evil" with no spiritual connection with God. This would mean all of us, too. This was never God's plan. His plan is for us to live in eternity, in goodness, with our loving Father.

Eve didn't do us girls any favours with her eating the fruit, but God's plan for our salvation is brilliant. Let me explain something which seems obvious to me but gets overlooked a lot. Adam was standing right there beside Eve when this whole scene with the devil was going down.[4]

It was Adam, not Eve, whom God told to not eat from the trees in the middle of the garden, but he didn't do anything except watch. Does Adam speak up and try to prevent anything from happening or suggest to Eve that maybe they should ask God about it? He was just as curious and at fault as Eve was, so he took a bite, too.

When God asks them, "Have you eaten from the tree that I commanded you not to eat from?"[5] Eve is silent for a bit, but Adam piped up and said, "The woman you put here with me—she gave me some fruit from the tree, and I ate it." Adam isn't only pointing the finger at Eve as the culprit but also at God for bringing *that* woman and giving her to him. He blames Eve, and he blames God. The birth of the blame-game. Evil had already slithered into the perfect garden.

In studying the Eve story, it is disturbing to discover the quick emergence of three evil dividers between God and us—fear, shame, and blame. When God asked Adam where he was (hiding behind a bush), Adams replied, *"I heard you in the garden, and I was afraid because I was naked; so I hid"* (Genesis 3:10, NIV).

This explains the whole condition of the human race—*I was naked and afraid, so I hid.* Fear and shame entered, and instead of seeking God, they turned away from Him by hiding. Adam and Eve didn't want to be with God anymore in the perfect garden, and this severed their relationship with Him. Our spiritual connection to God died at this moment as well. We were all separated from God.

This is where the dead spirit we have inside of us originates from. Hal Lindsey says it clearly in his book *The Liberation of Planet Earth*. I poured over this book when I first became a follower of Christ, along with C.S. Lewis' *Mere Christianity*. Both answered many questions I had.

"When man was created, he *did* have God's spiritual life resident within him, but when he sinned and turned his back on God, he lost that spiritual life. Now every man is born without it, and if he wants God to be his father for now and through eternity, he must have God's life put back into him sometime before he dies physically on this earth."[6]

I know God has a plan for all of us to be brought back into harmony with Him so we can again walk around His perfect garden talking with Him. One of my first questions to Him is going to be: Why put the trees there in the first place? God has said many times in Scripture that His ways are not our ways, so better to let it go for now until I see him.

COMPASSION FOR THE BROKEN-HEARTED

"Shout for joy, you heavens; rejoice, you earth; burst into song, you mountains! For the Lord comforts his people and will have compassion on his afflicted ones."

— ISAIAH 49:13, NIV

Jesus said right from the beginning He didn't come down to earth for those who have it all figured out (in their own minds) but for those of us who are broken to pieces.[7] That's me. Oh, hallelujah, I'm not left here to muck around in my own mess or to walk through the thick mud of the agony of loss, pain and shame—not to mention the terrible destroyers known as anxiety, jealousy, envy, hatred, gossip, adultery, addictions, and so on.

This is good, good news because I lived this way most of my life. I admit I still have a broken heart for our world, as beautiful as it is, but now I live with God near to me, so it doesn't seem so hopeless.

We can all look around the streets, office towers, back alleys, shopping malls and fancy restaurants of our own towns or cities and see all the broken people there. We see them also even in the churches all over the world. Being a follower of Jesus doesn't mean I'm exempt from the struggles and pain of this world, but it does mean I have somebody I can count on who loves me and comforts me in my pain right to the very end of my life. I have hope.

EVE

When I was getting near the end of writing this book, I was suddenly prompted to write about Eve, the first daughter of God and the first woman to have a relationship with God the Father. How glorious that must have been—to be in the Garden of Eden, the perfect place, with God. She was the only woman to experience a pure, unhindered relationship with Him.

How does Eve tie in with Jesus? I mentioned Jesus' big job on earth is to bring everyone back into harmony with God, back into a relationship with the Father like the first daughter of God had. Eve walked with Him, talked with Him, laughed with Him, told Him her problems, and asked Him for advice. She did life with Him. This is what she had with God, but unfortunately, she caused us not to have that relationship with Him.

God wants us to be like Eve and walk in the garden with Him again in perfect harmony. Oh my. Perfect harmony with God. This is why the story of Eve is so very important to be told. I can't write this book and not tell her story because it is the missing piece. Her story connects all of these stories I have shared about Jesus and the women He encountered and transformed while He walked the earth.

One day while I was walking through the woods, Jesus breathed into to me, saying;

"Women, I need to bring you back to the garden. Women, you need to come back to God and be back in harmony with Him. Women, wake

up. Follow Me. Come with Me to the garden. Come with Me to the garden and be Eve again. Be my beautiful Eve again."

That's the call.

Who was Eve in the garden? She was perfect in a perfect place. She had no guilt, rage, insecurity, shame, jealousy, or hate. She wasn't comparing herself, seeking approval, or trying to be somebody she wasn't. She was happy, joy-filled, loved, and adored. She was God's feminine design of beauty and perfection. This is how she was created.

Can you see her walking there in a tranquil, lush garden, the birds flapping and chirping, the animals lazing in the sun, butterflies fluttering about with vibrant blue and orange wings? She talked with Adam, and they laughed and shared each other. They loved each other without all the angst between men and women we carry with us today.

God was with Adam and Eve, and they were in a wonderous, pure relationship. He loved them, and they loved Him. Harmony. Do you think God was singing as He walked through the garden with them? I think you can be sure He was. His kids were with Him, and they were having so much fun in the perfect place in perfect harmony.

THE SINGING GOD

I started to write this poem several years ago when I first discovered The Singing God. I was prompted to finish it for this book:

> *Your very breath bends the ancient cedar trees,*
> *And melts away snow-capped mountains in a breeze.*
> *Your arms crash mighty waves on windswept shores,*
> *Your blazing eyes demand all stars and moon to glow.*
> *Your thoughts command the sun to heat our spinning globe,*
> *Your mightiness splits canyons in two, sets river waters aflow.*

Your fingers brush over misty valleys, such majesty they bring,
Yet, You gently settle me beneath Your calming wings,
wrap me in light, kiss me with delight, and sing over me,
when no one else does.

Your love breaks through my stubborn prison walls,
Your heart chases me to the cliff tops, Your love calls.
Your everlasting arms catch me when I hurl myself too deep.
Why do I look beyond your ways and walk this road so steep?
When my tarnished path gets thorny,
bloodied feet trudging despair,
As I look to another way,
all hope fades bleak in the dark night air.
Yet, You, O Yahweh, once more,
wrap me in light, kiss me with delight and sing over me,
when no one else does.

He sings over me when nobody else does. I used to believe the second part of this statement way before I believed the first part. I believed nobody sang over me, nobody loved me. Now, I know God sings over me. He spins and sings over me, twirling and spinning in absolute delight and abandonment. He isn't singing over me just to sing. He is singing and rejoicing over me because I said yes to His offer to save me.

He is mighty to save us—this makes God sing and dance. He reacts this way because He loves me. God's love letter to us, the Bible, says so. A whole book has been written just for us to tell us how much He loves us. He has a magnificent divine plan just for me and for you, too.

If there was only one woman left on earth—you—He would have still written this love letter and come up with a plan to save you. Sister, please don't walk away from the God who sings and spins over you. What delight He takes in you, your smiling angel face, your sweet singing voice, your wise twinkling eyes, every grey hair on your head, your many laugh lines, and your creative artist's hands.

What does it mean that He sings over me? It means He is so utterly pleased with me that only songs will express such love and delight!

NATURE SINGS GOD'S GLORY

Nature sings of God's glory, and so this is one way God sings over me.

Before I believed in Jesus, I didn't really think too much about nature or beauty. I liked a sunset like most people and noticed robins when they arrived in the spring. I was more annoyed with the snow and rain than to see anything wonderful in them. And the ocean made me seasick so no joy there.

When I said yes to Jesus, my heart for nature changed. The moment I asked Jesus to come into my heart, the sky didn't become a brilliant blue or the grass a shade of heavenly green that I'd never seen before, but the world around me did start to sing.

Steve and I saved up for a year to go to Africa on our honeymoon, and this is where I discovered birds. We saw all the magnificent animals Africa had to offer, but it was the exotic birds that captured my heart. When we returned home, I began to notice the exotic birds in the park near to our house. I didn't have to go all the way to Africa to see exquisite birdlife; they were right there in my own backyard all along.

We began hiking in the rainforest and coastal mountains a short drive from our doorstep. The light dappled upon the sword ferns and caused the ancient fir trees to glow. We walked through magical forests of giant maple trees dressed in moss and lichen. Flowers in our backyard seemed to take on a new dimension. Waves along the shore became a reflective, meditative place of peace and calmness so that, even in stormy weather, they beat like the Father's heart in soothing repetition. God seemed to be singing over me with the beauty of His creation.

I picked up a camera and began capturing the beauty I witnessed in the simplest of days. Then something interesting began to unfold. My nature photographs were accepted into a local "art in the garden" tour. Then I applied for a small show in a gallery and was accepted. Next, I began to submit my photographs to a professional photography association and received accreditations for several of my portfolios—nature, landscapes, wildlife, and botanicals.

I entered an image of a red maple tree into a national competition one year and won "Best in Class." I submitted some of my photographs and an article to a nature magazine and was published several times. I prayed and left each entry or submission in God's hands to do as He pleased. All by the grace of God.

TRULY SINGING

Nature is alive and shouting God's glory to us every day.

Jesus said something so funny the day He rode into Jerusalem on the colt just before going to the cross. The Pharisees were all bent out of shape because His followers were dancing and shouting as He rode by, so they asked Jesus to get His disciples to stop with all the noise and ruckus they were making. He replied, *"If they kept quiet, the stones along the road would burst into cheers!"* (Luke 19:40, NLT). Even the rocks sing of God's glory. I think it's funny and believe God has a fabulous sense of humour.

His creation is one of the ways God sings over us so we will not forget Him or the love and grace He has for us. Through the display of creation we come to know how much He adores and cherishes us.

Come back to God and be "Eve." Be like His first daughter: loved, adored, cherished, crowned, and sung over. Let Him sing and spin over you like you were always meant to be.

PRAY. WALK. LISTEN.

He didn't create this magnificent earth for Himself—He's already in the most magnificent place there is, Heaven, and someday we will be there, too. But for now, God created this stunning, magnificent place for us. Step out into the forests and the seashores and listen to His songs, the beating of His heart in the waves of the sea or the whisper of His voice through the tall pine trees.

Oftentimes, God will speak to me when I am out walking alone in nature. He speaks to some of my friends this way, too. Again, nothing is fancy or complicated—you could call this a simple prayer walk. Go for a walk. Have a talk. You don't need to talk out loud—just an internal heart-to-heart talk. Then listen for His singing.

SOMETHING TO PONDER

Do you want God to sing over you? Do you want to experience His presence and peace in your life? Do you want to hear His voice and His heart beating for you?

> *"Arise, my darling, my beautiful one, come with me. See! The winter is past; the rains are over and gone. Flowers appear on the earth; the season of singing has come, the cooing of doves is heard in our land."*

> — SONG OF SONGS 2:10-12, NIV

THE EVERLASTING GOD AND THE DAUGHTER AT THE TOMB

"Before the mountains were born or you brought forth the earth and the world, from everlasting to everlasting you are God."
— Psalm 90:2, NIV —

"One thing I ask from the Lord, this only do I seek: that I may dwell in the house of the Lord all the days of my life, to gaze on the beauty of the Lord and to seek him in his temple."
— Psalm 27:4, NIV —

MARY AT THE TOMB

*M*ary Magdalena was there the day Jesus was nailed to the cross. She watched Him bleed to death. Jesus—the one who freed her from seven demons, taught her about a new life she could have, laughed with her, enjoyed meals with her, and walked dusty Judean roads with her—was now dead and gone.

What now? She could think of nothing more in those early hours after His death than to be near Him, so she followed His body to the tomb to grieve Him there. Mary wept and watched as a huge stone was rolled into place shutting the tomb and His body into darkness forever.[1]

Mary waited through the sabbath day in disbelief and sorrow, but early the following day, she arrived back at the tomb, discovering the massive stone had been rolled away revealing an empty tomb. She ran to tell the disciples His body was gone.

In doubt, Peter and John charged out to have a look for themselves and soon discovered Mary's report was true. The only thing left inside the tomb was the linen Jesus had been wrapped in. They went back home while Mary lingered behind and wept some more. Not only had she just lost her beautiful teacher and friend, but now His body had been stolen. She took one last look into the empty tomb...

Oh, if only the guys had stuck around. Two beautiful white angels were sitting where Jesus' body had lain, and they spoke with Mary and asked why she was crying.

> *"They have taken my Lord away and I don't know where they have put him."*
>
> — JOHN 20:13, NIV

She turned around to leave, and encountered Jesus standing there beside her, but she didn't recognize Him and assumed He was the gardener. The man Jesus asked her the same questions as the angels— why are you crying, and who are you looking for?[2]

She pleaded with him to reveal where the body had been taken so she, herself, could go get it. Jesus said to her, "Mary."[3]

With the mention of her name, Mary immediately recognized Jesus and cried out to Him. She wanted to embrace Him, but He cautioned her not to cling to Him. He wasn't staying on earth. His mission wasn't complete yet, and He needed to return to Heaven to complete God's redemption plan to repair the breach between us and God.

"Mary, don't hold on to me now, for I haven't yet ascended to God, my Father. And he's not only my Father and God, but now he's your Father and your God! Now go to my brothers and tell them what I've told you, that I am ascending to my Father—and your Father, to my God—and your God!"

— JOHN 20:17, TPT

I want to jump up and down with glee over this because He honoured a woman with the most important message for all humanity: He is alive, and He has risen! Mary was the first person to see Jesus resurrected and the first person made aware of the final step to mend the brokenness between God and us. She is the first person commissioned to tell the world about seeing Him alive and risen.

Mary went to the disciples with the news: *"I have seen the Lord!"* (John 20:18, TPT). The first evangelist of the resurrection was a woman! And, it was a woman with a messy, broken past. Amazing!

Why was this honour given to a woman? I don't know exactly why, but I know God doesn't make mistakes. Did God give this honour to a woman because a woman (Eve) was the one who ate the fruit in the garden and got us in this mess in the first place? Perhaps.

We've really carried a heavy burden with that one, so honouring a woman with being the first to see the resurrected Saviour of the world is a loving way to show how important women are to God. We are not excluded from His grand plan.

In spite of all the pain, suffering and hatred we've endured, we are truly loved and adored by God, so He gave a woman this honour. He is the Everlasting God who has included women into His heavenly plans. We are not forgotten, tossed out, or excluded from eternity.

HIS SWORD OF GOOD WORDS

"God sends angels with special orders to protect you wherever you go, defending you from all harm."

— PSALM 91:11, TPT

I want to tell you of an experience I had when it became clear to me God will never leave us once we invite Him into our life. My mom was one of His daughters, and she was dying. It was the day she couldn't read anymore, another endless day my sister and I spent suspended in this place of cancer hell. The nurses said she only had a few days left to live, and it wouldn't be long. But it was. She stayed alive. While her heart kept beating on and on, her body was slowly shutting down, moment by moment, bit by bit.

Mom and I eventually shared the same faith—we both believed in our beautiful Jesus Christ. As I mentioned earlier, I didn't grow up in a Christian home, and my mother didn't become a believer until her late forties.

We grew stronger and closer as mother and daughter after I became a follower many years later, but it wasn't always like that. Before I knew Jesus, she really annoyed me because I was hurting, damaged, and messed up. I looked at her with unkind eyes, blaming her for the mess I was in. Well, who else? It couldn't be me doing all this damage, so it had to be my mother.

Poor moms get blamed for so much. I pulled an Adam and blamed her for my own messy life I created out of feeling unloved, ashamed, and insecure. My heart was hardened towards her, yet Jesus brought us back into a loving relationship with each other. He healed us and for the last eight years of her life, we shared the same love for Jesus and became really close friends. A miracle.

The day she lay so helpless and sick was the day she could no longer read, so I asked if she would like me to read the Bible to her.

"Oh, yes, I would love that."

"Where would you like me to start?"

"Psalm twenty-three."

I sat in the rocking chair in her bedroom at my sister's house, where she spent the last months of her life, and began to read. She recited the verses along with me, but after Psalm 23 was over, she said she was going to rest her eyes.

"Would you keep reading?" she asked.

Yes, of course.

It was around this time I felt a heaviness seep into the room. It darkened, and the air became like thick pea soup. The words on my tongue were like heavy molasses in my mouth. I felt like I was speaking in slow motion, the words barely leaking out. I knew I had to keep reading the words—God's words. Love wins.

Jesus help me.

I kept reading verses over her.

Keep reading, don't stop. Lord, help me read these words. Don't let me stop.

It was like white pasty glue now in my mouth, but I kept reading Psalm after Psalm. It seemed the minutes were actually hours as I sat in the chair, Bible in my lap, words barely audible, but somehow, I knew I had to keep reading His words—one syllable at a time.

King Jesus be here now. Fight for us. I put my trust in You to do battle for us now.

The Word of God is His Sword. The enemy did not want words spoken over God's daughter that day, and he wanted to shut me up.

What a creep.

I read for an hour or so, tongue thick and heavy, but somehow, I persevered with one phrase at a time. Eventually, the room cleared, light flooded back in through the windows again, and a lightness in the atmosphere arose around us. I knew it was okay to leave her there to sleep for a while. The heaviness had been lifted.

I curled up on the couch in my sister's living room and rested. I may have cried. God is good. Hallelujah! Jesus' love always wins. God's words are weapons that, when spoken, even by a fairly new believer like I was, have the power to chase out the enemy. Keep this in mind for yourself.

It would be a few more weeks before Mom would slip into a coma and then a few more until her body finally gave out. I was incredibly blessed to have been there with her that day to read the very words of God into her ears before she drifted off to sleep.

I will never forget this battle. I am glad it happened because it reminds me quite often that the enemy doesn't want any of us women to be with God—not today and certainly not in Heaven. What seems incredibly bold to me is satan still picks away at us even when we belong to God and are saved into eternity. It's like he doesn't get it. We belong to The Everlasting God! He's our dad and our dad isn't going to let anything come between us and Him. Nothing. This is His mighty promise to us in His love letter:

> "No power in the sky above or in the earth below—indeed, nothing in all creation will ever be able to separate us from the love of God that is revealed in Christ Jesus our Lord."

> — ROMANS 8:39, NLT

THE EVERLASTING GOD

"Do you not know? Have you not heard? The LORD is the everlasting God, the Creator of the end of the earth. He will not grow tired or weary, and his understanding no one can fathom."

— ISAIAH 40:28, NIV

The Everlasting God saved me from spending eternity in darkness without Him. Once I said yes to Jesus and let Him love me, that was when everything started to change for me. And it can change for you, too. He entered my life and began to tear down the old life. He unveiled my heart of iron and then began to rebuild, reshape and reconstruct the beautiful life He had planned for me.

Like He did for Mary, Jesus transformed my life. I am no longer sitting in the dark obsessed with trying to please others or seeking terrible ways to squelch the emptiness inside. I'm following Jesus, who is the light for this world, and I believe this is because He did for me what nobody else could—He gave me my life back.

He promises I will be in paradise with The Everlasting God. Knowing this one truth alone shows me how much God loves me. This one truth gives me purpose, tells me I matter, shows me how important I am, and explains the reason why I am here. The reason I am here is this: All along it was God's plan that I would exist and be here—right here and right now—at this very moment in time.

The Almighty God of the Universe planned for me! He calls me His daughter, and He says He loves me lavishly—not just a bit of love but an extravagant amount of it.

"How great is the love the Father has lavished on us, that we should be called children of God! And that is what we are!"

— 1 JOHN 3:1, NIV

Then.

"Before I'd ever seen the light of day, the number of days you planned for me were already recorded in your book."

— PSALM 139:16, TPT

How could I possibly doubt the Everlasting God who wrote these promises? He promises the exact same blessings for you...if you would only let Him love you. It is by no mistake you are curious about God and beginning a pilgrimage to discover who you are, why you were born, and what purpose you have while on this earth. Everybody wants to know these things, and God wants you to know them, too. *God wants you to know Him.*

ETERNITY IN OUR HEARTS

"He has made everything beautiful in its time. He has also set eternity in the human heart; yet no one can fathom what God has done from beginning to end."

— ECCLESIASTES 3:11, NIV

Everlasting to everlasting, this is how long God's words last. His words are promises which last forever. He breathed them into our hearts so we would know God forever. His Word is complete, beautiful, and true.

I have been reading Scripture for a few decades now, and from the time I picked up that little blue Bible until now, I still find it so awe-inspiring yet mysterious. Words I read twenty years ago still sing in my heart. Whenever I think about my mom or write in my journal about her, Ecclesiastes 3:11 comes quickly to mind and, along with it, tears—indeed, delightful tears. *"He has made everything beautiful in its time.*" I think this is true about us all. God says we are beautiful in our time.

Then there are words I read years ago—just glossing over them without a second glance—until the perfect time when they come alive and sing to my heart. Take for example this verse in the Old Testament: *"Let the beloved of the LORD rest secure in him, for he shields him all day long, and the one the LORD loves rests between his shoulders"* (Deuteronomy 33:11, NIV). He promises me a special resting place between His almighty shoulders. This verse has come delightfully alive to me today with the promise that I am riding upon His shoulders like a little girl up on her daddy's shoulders protected from the danger, chaos, and battle taking place below.

TRULY EVERLASTING

"Jesus, the Anointed One, is always the same—yesterday, today, and forever."

— HEBREWS 13:8, TPT

The Everlasting God promises He will exist forever and never change. This means His promises to us will last until the end of time. If He says we will be in paradise with Him, this is the truth, and we can believe and trust He will do this for us. He doesn't back out of His promises like us humans do.

I don't want a God who is here today and gone tomorrow. I have had enough of that with people. He is The Everlasting God who—through His steadfast love, overflowing grace, mercy, and wondrous faith—has provided a way for us all to be with Him in paradise.

Today, when I sat with the Bible on my lap, I wondered how old it was. When was it written? It was written way before Jesus' time two thousand years ago, and it was also written after His time on earth, too. I did a bit of digging and discovered scholars traditionally believe the first five books of the Bible were attributed to Moses' authorship, and he lived between 1350–1230 BC.[4] The events Moses writes about in Genesis 1–11 occurred way before 2000 BC.[5] All of this to say, the old part of the God's words are over 3,300 years old, and the new part of His words are around two thousand years old. And yet they still speak, sing, and shout out to me today. These words are the living words of God!

His words melt my heart and make me want to be a better person. They spark my heart into action: I don't want to be useless or without purpose. Instead, I want to be useful and to share the gifts God has breathed into me. His words touch me with tears at times, laughter at other times, and, with a wide-opened heart smile, they make me want to dance all around the house.

It's a new day. I get to wake up every day with new possibilities and to seek new adventures with God.

Sometimes, the words from Scripture invoke anger and frustration when God's ways don't line up with mine. Then I need to pray and seek understanding. His thoughts and ways are not like ours—His are so much higher. I am grateful for this because I don't want to entrust my heart, spirit, and soul to someone who thinks and acts like I do, or worse.

I want to trust Someone who has a much higher way and standard than I have...and still promises I get to sit on His daddy shoulders and rest there in His love.

PRAY TO MELT OUR HEARTS

Jesus can heal your relationship with anyone into a loving relationship—like He did for my mom and me. I don't know how He does it, but He does, and that's all I needed to know.

You've probably figured out by now that you're the one who is going to need to take the first step towards changing your relationship with another person. You only need to take one baby step at a time, though.

First though, if you haven't asked Jesus to step into your heart and life and take over, this will be your biggest step to take. Once you've asked Him for this, everything falls into place, and your heart will melt for others, including your mom (or whomever troubles you).

A small poem prayer for eternity:

O Jesus, build in me faith and trust
So there is no decay or rust;
Instead bless me with a "forever us."

SOMETHING TO PONDER

Have you been thinking about your relationship with your own mother lately? Have you pointed fingers at her for your messy life, like I did? I did something powerful on the last day of the year my mother passed away. If you are having a particularly tough time, this is something you may want to do, too.

It was the last day of 2006. I was up to my armpits in struggles, stress, cancer, death, and it seemed like I was expected to just get back to normal after losing her. *Huh?* She was one of the most influential women in my life. She was beautiful and had a childlike faith I admired. She had a great sense of humour, too. Oh, if I could only be as joyful and funny as she was, giggling uncontrollably with her special friend, Marg, who lived down the lane from her house. I laughed along with them, not because I found them funny, but because they laughed so hard at their own silly jokes, which I didn't get. Their laughter made me laugh. Oh, Mom and Marg, I know you are both with Him now, and I hope you are both making Jesus laugh so hard—as much as you made me laugh.

During that time, I was wondering, *What can I do to get rid of sadness and struggles of this year? How can I release everything that has happened? I will place it at Jesus' feet and let him sweep it all away.* Early in the evening, on the dining room table, I placed a big piece of art paper along with a supply of crayons and coloured pens. And then I began to draw on it throughout the evening.

I am not an illustrator but a photographer, so my drawings were rudimentary and simple, but this didn't matter as they were symbolic of the season I was going through. Whatever came out on the paper was meant to be there. I wrote words, too. I included the verse about everything being beautiful in its time. I printed out a small prayer, and then I wrote these words:

> *"There is a time for everything, and a season for every activity under the heavens: a time to be born and a time to die, a time to plant and a time to uproot, a time to kill and a time to heal, a time to tear down and a time to build, a time to weep and a time to laugh, a time to mourn and a time to dance..."*
>
> — ECCLESIASTES 3:1-4, NIV

(And you thought The Byrd's came up with these words for their hit single "Turn! Turn! Turn!" Nope, these words are straight out of God's love letter to us!)

Late into the night I built a fire in the backyard, and while I prayed and asked Jesus to take all these things onto Himself, I held the poster over the fire and watched it burn. It became ashes. Out of the ashes came peace.

> *"Surely your goodness and love will follow me all the days of my life, and I will dwell in the house of the Lord forever."*
>
> — PSALM 23:6, NIV

THE JUBILEE GOD AND THE LOST PRINCESS

"He will give a crown of beauty for ashes, a joyous blessing instead of mourning, festive praise instead of despair."
— Isaiah 61:3, NLT —

"Let's prepare a great feast and celebrate. For this beloved son of mine was once dead, but now he's alive again. Once he was lost, but now he is found!' And everyone celebrated with overflowing joy."
— Luke 15:23-24, TPT —

THE STORY OF THE LOST PRINCESS

*T*here once was a princess who wanted her freedom. She'd had enough with all the pressures and troubles in her life. She felt certain that if she could get away from everything associated with the pain, heartache and stupid things she had done in her past, she would be free and happy. So, she ran away to a nearby city. But the Father King secretly followed her there to make sure she got to where she was going safely. Then He waited for her. He waited for forty years.

This nearby city suited the princess quite well because she could disappear into the crowds of people and do her own thing. She found a way to make a living, pushing paper around a desk for a big corporation, and there she met some friends just like herself. They had all run away too and were looking for freedom from their painful past. They lived wildly and were free to do whatever they wanted.

The princess really liked these new people who seemed to like her back. Oh, how they all laughed at their antics, danced until the drugs wore off, sang drunken songs in bars, and staggered around back alleys at 3 a.m. They spent their meagre wages on methods to help themselves feel better and to make the pain and emptiness go away. The princess disappeared into dark drinking parlours, all-night party houses, and unrestrained relationships with immoral men.

All the while, the Father King continued to wait for her. Sometimes, when she was doing something dangerous or stupid, he would send in an angel of protection to illuminate a better way for her. But mostly the Father King waited for her.

After a time, the princess ended up in a dark, cold dungeon where there was very little light. She stayed there for a while, and it became evident in this place that nobody was coming to save her anytime soon. All her friends had vanished, and the uncaring men were nowhere to be found.

The princess had gotten what she was looking for. She had her freedom to do whatever she wanted, and she had, indeed, disappeared, but now...she was alone with a dead, numb heart. She wasn't happy and free at all but a prisoner in the dark with a gaping emptiness deep in her spirit.

The Father King did not leave the princess alone in the dungeon but instead instructed an angel to drop a seed of light into the girl's heart. And then he made it grow and soften by dropping another seed and another drop of light and another seed. And so on.

One of those seeds was a small book he had written just for her. She picked it up and read it, wondering where it had come from. While she read the book, her father increased her curiosity, and she thought of him for the first time in a long time, so she began to cry. She thought to herself, "I know I have made big mistakes with the awful way I have been living... Oh, if only I could go home and see my daddy; maybe I would be happy again."

The Father King heard her sorrowful plea, and he opened the door to the dungeon and left it open until, finally, the princess slowly walked out into the daylight. She decided, in the light, she would begin a pilgrimage to find her father.

The day came when the princess, though still far off, was walking towards her father with hope in her heart. This was so pleasing to her father, and he began to move toward her. Even while she was still off in the distance, the Father King was singing and dancing because his princess was on her way home.

As she walked along the path, there were many crossroads she could take, but her Father King loved her so much he illuminated the right way. Soon, she came to a hill and climbed up until she found a wooden cross, radiant in light, with a man hanging upon it. When she looked up, a single drop of his blood spilled upon the princess' forehead, and she began to weep.

The man looked into her eyes and said, "I've been sent to bring you home because your father loves you deeply. I've taken your place on this cross and already paid for your bad choices so that now, together, we can walk to your Father. That single drop of my blood will wash you clean and set you free from your misery because our Father King has made it so. There is a better way dear one; I am that way. All you need to do now is to believe in me, say yes, and let me love you."

"But I've done so many stupid and evil things. I don't think he's going to want me, and besides, you can surely see I'm a bit of a mess. I'm not princess material anymore. I've made such a disaster of my life."

"Don't worry about all that. The father knows your heart, and it's all he's interested in. He doesn't see any of your mucky mess or wrong-doings anymore. He wants you with him in his wonderful house. In fact, he already has a room there waiting for you. Let me love you and guide you while you make your pilgrimage to him."

The lost princess cried out, "What? That's all I have to do."

"Yes, my way is easy, and my burden is light. You will find rest and peace when you travel the way with me."

While the princess was still far off, walking with the man from the cross, the Father King was spinning with delight and calling to his servants, "Quick! Get her tiara ready, her robe and ring too. My daughter was dead and lost, but now she is found. She's alive. She's alive. My princess will be with me in eternity! Let's have a jubilee feast tonight and celebrate my daughter. Get her favourite band ready, and tell them to play her favourite song. Let us dance and sing. My daughter is alive! My son is bringing her home."

The Father King ran to his daughter with the tiara, robe, and ring in hand. He wrapped his arms around her and gently embraced her head to his chest. "It's all okay now. I've got you my daughter. I've got you. You're home."

All the Father King's sons and daughters were dancing and singing, and His angels were cheering with glee.

A JUBILEE CELEBRATION

> "That's the way God responds every time one lost sinner repents and turns to him. He says to all his angels, 'Let's have a joyous celebration, for that one who was lost I have found!'"

— LUKE 15:10, TPT

A jubilee is a grand party. Whenever the Queen of England reaches a significant milestone for sitting on the British throne, she throws herself a celebration. To date, she's had a Silver, Golden, Diamond, and Sapphire Jubilee, celebrating her monarchy throughout the British Commonwealth.[1]

The Jubilee Year described in the Old Testament of the Bible is a different party altogether. It was a celebration for when freedom and restoration was given by God, and so the people in those days celebrated with His favour for a full year. God declared on the fiftieth year,[2] the land will rest, all slaves will be set free, and every debt will be forgiven.

The year of Jubilee was one of the ways God provided justice back in those ancient days. When debt was forgiven and people were freed, it kept the wealthy from accumulating more wealth and the poor from getting poorer, and it ensured those who were slaves would be set free from their chains one day. Everyone was allowed to return to the land they had lost to others because of debt. Nobody owed anybody anything anymore. Slaves who had lost their life to a debt they could never repay were, graciously, freed.

The land rested for the entire year so that the following year, it would be more abundant than ever before. God promised His supernatural favour in these celebratory years by pouring out His grace upon the people He loved. Nobody went hungry, and everyone enjoyed a debt-free life once again.

THE JUBILEE GOD

The Jubilee God is a celebration, and He also celebrates.

Everything He created is a celebration. Here are just a few simple—yet simply breathtaking—examples:

- While walking in the forest last week, a barred owl landed on a branch and posed for us. After twenty minutes, she took flight towards us and flew past our faces just ten feet away. The details of her feathers and the sparks in her eyes were unforgettable.

- One day this past summer, during a magenta sunset, the crystal blue waves of the ocean pounded upon the shore, mesmerizing us with the rhythm of the Father's heart.
- Yesterday, four bald eagles glided by our deck, dancing, squealing, and spiralling through the air in their annual mating ritual, right before our eyes.
- Earlier this year, our great-niece and great-nephew were born with perfect, tiny fingernails and baby-hair eyelashes.
- Early in the summer, the first strawberry of the season gleamed bright red and spilled forth a juicy sweet flavour beyond description.
- Several years back, a chameleon in the Namib desert changed itself from beige to black right in front of our very eyes, but only on one side of its body.

These are celebrations!

He is celebration because He has given us this magnificent place to live while we pilgrimage with Him. All too often, we ignore His magnificent beauty and think, *Well, no big deal. Too busy. I gotta be somewhere. Yeah, yeah whatever. So what, a bunch of waves.* Hands brushing away the view. Then, doesn't our life look exactly how we act and think—a nonchalant, mediocre, dreary existence instead of the rich, abundant, adventurous story He has promised us?

Our attitude can easily be remedied with Jesus, so not all is lost.

How much more would The Jubilee God celebrate the return of one of His lost daughters into His loving home?

> *"In the same way, I tell you, there is rejoicing in the presence of the angels of God over one sinner who repents."*

> — LUKE 15:10, NIV

JESUS IS JUBILEE

Jesus stood up in the synagogue when he first began His mission on earth and announced He was the Jubilee, the year of favour. This is what He said:

> *"The Spirit of the Lord is upon me, and he has anointed me to be hope for the poor, freedom for the broken-hearted, and new eyes for the blind, and to preach to prisoners, 'You are set free!' I have come to share the message of Jubilee, for the time of God's great acceptance has begun."*

> — LUKE 4:18-19, TPT

Jesus is our jubilee because every day He brings liberty to those who are chained up with a broken heart; hope to those who have none; and sight to those who haven't been able to see light for a very long time. He brings love, forgiveness, and acceptance loosening the knots tied in the hearts of women all over the world.

Jesus represents a jubilee because He came to earth to give us freedom and restoration with God. He paid your debts and set you straight with God, and you are now free to be you. With no debt to worry about for the rest of your life, you are free to fly in the story of who you really are. When Jesus sets you free to fly—then *fly*. When He sets you free to sing—sing. When He sets you free to dance—dance. He will change the very essence of your heart.

GOD CELEBRATES

This is how God celebrates. Whenever one more of His lost princess-daughters is saved into His Kingdom, He and all of Heaven sing and dance.

He celebrates with us another way, too. He wants our life to be stellar here on earth while we are on our pilgrimage with Him. Everything true, noble, right, pure, lovely, admirable, excellent, and praiseworthy[3] is from God, and He gives us these things if we trust in Him. He wants us to shine for Him so others will want to know Him, too. Jesus' job here on earth is to bring all of us back into a relationship with God. This is why He came to earth—that not one of us would be left behind. We will all get to celebrate the Jubilee.

"He has taken me to the banquet hall, and his banner over me is love."

— SONG OF SONGS 2:4, NIV

COME TO THE JUBILEE

Are you walking an uneven path of hopelessness, not wanting to be alone anymore? Are you attempting to leave your shattered life but are afraid? Is your beautiful soul drowning in muddied, sin-soaked waters, rusting your heart into immovable parts? Not even a child's warm hand in yours, a dog's soft nose on your cheek, or the melody of triumphant music can crack a smile on your lonesome face? Are you this far gone?

Do you believe you can climb out of your pile of ashes?

Sooty ashes cling, and you can't seem to be scrubbed free from them. In the fiery circle, throw your tarnished shackles down and step out of the pile of ash swirling around you—making breath impossible, life miserable. Grab hold of the hands of Jesus. Let the ashes of your life be carried away by the wild wind of The Jubilee God, as you walk away from the fiery circle.

Come to your Jubilee at the foot of the ancient holy cross. Come and exchange your ashes for a crown of beauty there.

And then Jesus will ignite your life, set a crown upon your precious head and say: "This is your Jubilee."

The Father King steps down from His throne. He begins to sing and spin as all his princess-daughters begin to enter in.

He sings a message for you:

Oh joy! My daughter is coming home. My angels are waiting to dance and sing of her sweet return. Everyone, get the wine ready. Put on your best clothes. Get the band ready with her favourite song. Get her robe and crown ready. Get ready to dance. Let's have a feast and celebrate. My daughter is found, and she is on her way home to Me.

CROWN OF BEAUTY FOR ASHES

God promises us a crown of beauty for our ashes not only for eternity but while we are still here on earth. As His daughter, this is my crown: He uses all the good, ugly, bad, horrible, and painful things from my past for His good purposes.

I'm getting closer and closer to fitting into the princess crown He has placed upon my head. You see, it's tilted on my head and a bit wobbly, so it tumbles off all too easily while I'm still learning how to wear it. It slips off my head and down my back while I try to grab it. He catches it just before it smashes to the ground and sets it back on top of my undeserving head as I begin, one more time, to walk along His lightened path towards a beautiful eternity.

PRAY. SING. DANCE.

A small worship poem dropped into my heart for you. Pray it out loud. Dance it. Sing it. Believe it.

I am your beautiful crowned daughter,
who You are pleased with.
I am strong, brave,
and courageous in Your awesome power.

With You, I can move a mountain.
With You, I can scale a wall.

"They will sparkle in his land like jewels on a crown. How attractive and beautiful they will be!"

— ZECHARIAH 9:16–17, NIV

SOMETHING TO PONDER

What if you could come to the Jubilee? What if you could come to the dance? What if the band at the dance was playing your song? Would you dance? Would you celebrate? The band has your song. Would you dance there with the God of Jubilee?

Do you believe God is in Heaven now, patiently waiting for you to say yes to Him? Do you believe you are one of His lost princess-daughters?

Are you willing to leave the ashes of your past for the beauty of a new way?

Let Jesus love you.

Let Him be your new way.

EPILOGUE

LETTING THE BIRD FLY

"They will rise up on soaring wings and fly like eagles."
— Isaiah 40:31, TPT —

*"Place your hands of strength and favor upon me , for I've made my
choice to follow your ways. I wait for your deliverance, O Lord, for
your words thrill me like nothing else! Invigorate my life so that I can
praise you even more, and may your truth be my strength! I'll never
forget what you've taught me, Lord, but when I wander off and lose
my way, come after me, for I am your beloved!"*
— Psalm 119:176, TPT —

*W*hen I go to the C & B club (a local soup kitchen) to
serve breakfast to the street people, I know I am
supposed to be there to help out, and besides, this is something God
has asked me to do, so I better do it. Sometimes, I admit, I don't want
to go. For example, one Saturday in late November last year, I wanted
to stay home.

I didn't want to see the broken people and the children coming for a pancake or two because their dad can't feed them at home. I didn't want to see the drug addict who can't stop swaying back and forth, back and forth, back and forth, holding his head in his grubby hands, nails filthy with debris and black dirt. I didn't want to look into a young woman's face and see her teeth already rotted to stubs, eyes dead, and skin sallow or worse, full of open sores. I didn't want to see it. *Please, Lord, not today.*

It was a cold rainy day, too, with bleak winter clouds pouring out cold droplets of rain. This meant many would be coming to get some warm food and to drink hot coffee. It meant many of the volunteers might not show up. Since it is close to Christmas, they might opt for the shopping mall or Christmas craft fair instead. But again, He asked me to go so I knew it would be better if I showed up.

I prayed all the way to the building. *LORD, please, do I have to do this today? Can't I stay home?*

No.

Then I bargain with God. *Well, if I have to go, can I just scrub dishes instead? I feel too weak to serve the druggies today.* I had secretly brought a pair of rubber gloves, thinking I could just scrub dishes if He lets me. I have the rubber gloves, just in case.

In that moment, I was reminded that Jesus went to the cross. He basically asked God, Must I go through with this?[1] Turns out, He did. And so there I was—I couldn't even serve a few meals to some starving, needy people. Didn't He die for me, a needy one indeed? *Okay. Okay. I better stop complaining and stop asking for the lamest thing ever, purely out of laziness and wanting to stay cozy and safe. In my comfort zone.*

Then God nudged me with a thought. I had been prayer journaling a few months ago when He dropped into my heart a strong message that it was time for me to step out with Him and get uncomfortable.

Oh. That's right.

The building was jammed. It was the busiest I'd ever seen it. People were lined up down the hall and out the door to get some warm food. Servers were barrelling passed with food, coffee pots, and juice jugs. It was quite a madhouse! There was no more pleading with God for comfort. There was no turning back and running out the door to my car to escape. I jumped in. It was full-on serving. As soon as a fellow or gal finished their food, we would urge them to move on because the line-up outside was growing in the cold November rain. There was no time to chit chat with each other, only to say hello to the customers and, *"Can I get you some coffee, a full breakfast, sir or dear?"* Usually they were thankful for the food and warm liquid, sometimes not. But that's okay.

The building was jammed. It was the busiest I'd ever seen it. People were lined up down the hall and out the door to get some warm food. Servers were barrelling passed with food, coffee pots, and juice jugs. It was quite a madhouse! There was no more pleading with God for comfort. There was no turning back and running out the door to my car to escape. I jumped in. It was full-on serving. As soon as a fellow or gal finished their food, we would urge them to move on because the line-up outside was growing in the cold November rain. There was no time to chit chat with each other, only to say hello to the customers and, *"Can I get you some coffee, a full breakfast, sir or dear?"* Usually they were thankful for the food and warm liquid, sometimes not. But that's okay.

Forty-five minutes into the madness, I noticed Lorraine. She had been doing dishes, washing and scrubbing the whole shift, and I knew she had a tender back. The sink is built to the wrong height, so it is uncomfortable leaning over it.

"Do you need a break from the dishes?"

"Yes, please. My back is killing me."

I ran to the car and grabbed my gloves. Then I jumped in, taking over the dish-washing work. She could serve the folks instead and give her back a break.

The dishes had piled up, and they didn't stop coming. As soon as ten plates were clean, fifteen appeared in their place. *LORD, give me strength. Help me do this.* I told myself to think of Brother Lawrence, a dear saint from years ago who is well known for his humble service and deep communion with God. I tried to keep his ways in mind in everything I was doing, reminding myself to do it for the love of God:

> "I turn over my little omelet in the frying pan for the love of God. When it is finished, if I have nothing to do, I prostrate myself on the ground and adore my God from whom the grace came to make it."[2]

> — BROTHER LAWRENCE

But the dishes were relentless, and the scraping bucket and the slop buckets were full. Somebody was kindly keeping a scrap container for the street dogs. Dogs are homeless too in our town. Such a sweet act of kindness and I wish I'd thought of it.

More dishes. *Brother Lawrence.* For the rest of the shift I was on the dishes, just what I had prayed for. *Ha.* Yeah, but I didn't think it would be this hard.

I'm a good worker; I can do physical work. I grew up working on a farm, feeding animals, weeding gardens, picking stones out of fields, washing clothes in the old-fashioned wringer washer, and whatnot. Even though I'm weak and skinny, I can work hard.

Brother Lawrence and his disposition was continually on my mind while I scraped and scrubbed. More people came through the door. There's a fight in the hallway. Somebody threw a fit in the dining hall and had to be taken out. Fighting of any kind is not allowed. Neither is sharing your faith.

Hmmm...why is that?

It was getting close to 11:30, and food was getting scarce. The sausages and eggs were dwindling and then gone. The pancakes and toast were the only food items left in the building. A lady saw a half-eaten sausage in the scrap bucket for the street dogs—she grabbed it, washed it under the tap, and ate it herself.

That's okay. It was meant for her anyway.

As the crowd began to lessen, the dishes continued to pile up and the clean-up didn't end. There were twenty or so hungry customers still to feed. Some lingered to stay warm; some kept their heads hung low, dozing in a warm place. We let them be.

"There's a bird up there! It's stuck up there on the window ledge," somebody yelled. There was. A sparrow had flown into the dining hall.

Coffee stopped being served. Pancakes were left on the griddle to burn. Dishes were left to soak and taps shut off. Those with their heads resting on the table or in their hands lifted up their eyes to see what was going on.

The bird flapped against the windowpane, desperate for the sky. The windows were high up the wall along the top of the ceiling, narrow and hard to reach. Someone grabbed a ladder from the storage room in the hallway. Another fellow grabbed a long, twirling device used for cranking open the window. We were all watching, mesmerized. Even the homeless and the drug addicts were watching intently while the bird flapped about for freedom.

She could see the sky, but she couldn't fly into it.

We were all gasping, *"The bird, the bird. Oh no, it's trapped."* My fear was the bird would perish there, inside, stuck in a place it's not meant to be—like so many people today. So many are stuck in a life, body, or mind where they were never intended to be. God never intended His children to be stuck in those lives they are living.

The guy with the twirling window device managed to crank the window open, but the bird wasn't set free right away. It still had to find its own way to the open space. We were all breathless, watching as it moved along the windowpane with the gentle encouragement of a broom. Finally, it reached the open sky and flew to freedom. Never looking back.

During that moment at the C & B club, we were all the same—food servers, church volunteers, homeless people, prostitutes, cooks, meth addicts, dishwashers, and, sadly, more eastside women. We were all hoping for the very same thing: freedom for the trapped bird. Freedom for each other? Freedom for ourselves?

Aren't we all the same with the same desire then—hoping for freedom? Freedom from our tied-up, trapped hearts and lives... The freedom Jesus lovingly gives us, if we let Him.

NOTES

1. THE AVAILABLE GOD AND THE BLEEDING WOMAN

1. Mother Teresa and Brother Roger, Seeking the Heart of God: Reflections On Prayer (New York, NY: HarperCollins Publishers, 1992), 16.
2. See Luke 10:25-37.
3. Jesus looked at them intently and said, "Humanly speaking, it is impossible. But not with God. Everything is possible with God." Mark 10:27 NLT
4. A Woman's Choice, Preface, Preface copyright 1993 by Eugenia Price, The Eugenia Price Treasury of Faith, A Main Street Book, Published by Doubleday

2. THE RESCUING GOD AND THE WOMAN AT THE WELL

1. Disapproval woman married more than three times: Page 1034, New Bible Commentary, 21st Century Edition, Edited by G.J. Wenham, J.A. Motyer, D.A. Carson, and R.T. France
2. Babul, Denna D., and Karin Luise. The Fatherless Daughter Project: Understanding Our Losses and Reclaiming Our Lives (New York: Avery, 2016), Page 170.

3. THE UNFAILING GOD AND THE SLEEPING DAUGHTER

1. The word translated *little girl* has the same affectionate tone to it as calling a child a "lamb" in English. Page 960, New Bible Commentary, 21st Century Edition, Edited by G.J. Wenham, J.A. Motyer, D.A. Carson, and R.T. France

4. THE CHASING GOD AND THE USED DAUGHTER

1. National Center for PTSD, Julie Whealin, Ph. D. https://web.archive.org/web/20090730101002/http://www.ptsd.va.gov/public/pages/child-sexual-abuse.asp
2. "Do not have sexual relations with your brother's wife, for this would violate your brother." Leviticus 18:16 NLT

3. Whatever happened to Herodias and Salome. Never Thirsty. https://www. neverthirsty.org/bible-qa/qa-archives/question/what-ever-happened-to-herodias- and-salome/

4. What girls receive from a good father: Page 127 & 128, The Fatherless Daughter Project, Denna D. Babul, RN, and Karin Luise, PhD.

5. The Lord is good to all; he has compassion on all he has made. Psalm 145:9 NIV

6. When Jesus overheard this, he spoke up and said, "Healthy people don't need to see a doctor, but the sick will go for treatment." Then he added, "Now you should go and study the meaning of the verse: I want you to show mercy, not just offer me a sacrifice. For I have come to invite the outcasts of society and sinners, not those who think they are already on the right path." Matthew 9:12-13 TPT

5. THE WARRIOR GOD AND MARY'S SEVEN DEMONS

1. Eldredge, John and Stasi, Captivating: Unveiling the Mystery of a Woman's Soul (Nashville, TN Thomas Nelson), 86.

2. Eldredge, John and Stasi, Captivating: Unveiling the Mystery of a Woman's Soul (Nashville, TN Thomas Nelson), 86.

3. See Ezekiel 28:12-14, NIV.

4. See Isa 14:13-14, NIV.

5. See Revelation 20:2-3.

6. He is faithful to all his promises and loving towards all He has made. Psalm 145:13b NIV

7. https://www.biblicalarchaeology.org/daily/people-cultures-in-the-bible/people- in-the-bible/was-mary-magdalene-wife-of-jesus-was-mary-magdalene-a- prostitute/

8. All have turned away, they have together become worthless; there is no one who does good, not even one. Romans 3:12 NIV

9. Then, looking into Thomas' eyes, he said, "Put your finger here in the wounds of my hands. Here—put your hand into my wounded side and see for yourself. Thomas, don't give in to your doubts any longer, just believe!" Then the words spilled out of his heart—"You are my Lord, and you are my God!" John 20:27-28 TPT

10. But the Holy Spirit produces this kind of fruit in our lives: love, joy, peace, patience, kindness, goodness, faithfulness, gentleness, and self-control. There is no law against these things! Galatians 5:22 & 23 NLT

6. THE PRISON-BUSTING GOD AND THE CROOKED WOMAN

1. See Luke 13:11.

2. See Matthew 11:28-30.

7. THE INVISIBLE GOD AND THE WIDOW WITH TWO COINS

1. Let everyone thank God, for he is good, and he is easy to please! His tender love for us continues on forever! Psalm 136:1 TPT
2. The one who doesn't love has yet to know God, for God is love. 1 John 4:8 TPT
3. "The virgin will conceive and give birth to a son, and they will call him Immanuel" (which means "God with us") Matthew 1:23 TPT

8. THE CATCHING GOD AND THE CAUGHT WOMAN

1. The Phrase Finder: https://www.phrases.org.uk/meanings/sticks-and-stones-may-break-my-bones.html
2. "In the Law Moses commanded us to stone such women." John 8:5 and "If a man commits adultery with another man's wife—with the wife of his neighbor—both the adulterer and the adulteress are to be put to death." Leviticus 20:10 NIV

9. THE UNSTOPPABLE GOD AND THE WIDOW OF NAIN

1. Anne Lamott, Hallelujah Anyway: Rediscovering Mercy (New York, NY: Random House Large Print, 2017) 99.
2. Definition of Hope. https://www.dictionary.com/browse/hope?s=t

10. THE ILLUMINATING GOD AND THE TRAVELING WOMEN

1. See 2 Corinthians 5:17.

11. THE SPILLING GOD AND A SINFUL WOMAN

1. Page 161, One Thousand Gifts, Ann Voskamp, ©2010 Ann Morton Voskamp, Published by Zondervan
2. Psalm 65:9 NLT
3. Description of shame, Page 1, The Persistence of Shame Following Sexual Abuse: A Longitudinal Look at Risk and Recovery, Candice Feiring, Lynn S. Taska, The College of New Jersey
4. Luke 7:47
5. Luke 7:48 & 50

12. THE SINGING GOD AND THE FIRST DAUGHTER

1. God saw all that he had made, and it was very good. And there was evening, and there was morning—the sixth day.| Genesis 1:31 NIV
2. "Did God really say, 'You must not eat from any tree in the garden'?" Genesis 3:1 "You will not certainly die," the serpent said to the woman. "For God knows that when you eat from it your eyes will be opened, and you will be like God, knowing good and evil." Genesis 3: 1 & 4 NIV
3. And the Lord God commanded the man, "You are free to eat from any tree in the garden; but you must not eat from the tree of the knowledge of good and evil, for when you eat from it you will certainly die. Genesis 2:16-17 NIV
4. See Genesis 3:6, NIV.
5. See Genesis 3:11.
6. Page 55, The Liberation of Planet Earth, Hal Lindsey © 1974 The Zondervan Corporation Grand Rapids, Michigan
7. Jesus answered them, "Healthy people don't need a doctor —sick people do. I have come to call not those who think they are righteous, but those who know they are sinners and need to repent." Luke 5:31&32 NLT

13. THE EVERLASTING GOD AND THE DAUGHTER AT THE TOMB

1. See Matthew 27:61.
2. See John 20:15.
3. See John 20:16.
4. Page 22 & 55, Moses' lifetime (1350-1230 BC) and Authorship, New Bible Commentary, 21st Century Edition, Edited by G.J. Wenham, J.A. Motyer, D.A. Carson and R.T. France;
5. Page 22, Old Testament Chronological Outline, New Bible Commentary, 21st Century Edition, Edited by G.J. Wenham, J.A. Motyer, D.A. Carson and R.T. France;

14. THE JUBILEE GOD AND THE LOST PRINCESS

1. https://en.wikipedia.org/wiki/Sapphire_Jubilee_of_Elizabeth_II
2. Consecrate the fiftieth year and proclaim liberty throughout the land to all its inhabitants. It shall be a jubilee for you; each of you is to return to your family property and to your own clan. The fiftieth year shall be a jubilee for you; do not sow and do not reap what grows of itself or harvest the untended vines. For it is a jubilee and is to be holy for you; eat only what is taken directly from the fields. "'In this Year of Jubilee everyone is to return to their own property. Leviticus 25:10-12 NIV

3. Finally, brothers and sisters, whatever is true, whatever is noble, whatever is right, whatever is pure, whatever is lovely, whatever is admirable—if anything is excellent or praiseworthy—think about such things. 9Whatever you have learned or received or heard from me, or seen in me—put it into practice. And the God of peace will be with you. Philippians 4:8 & 9 NIV

EPILOGUE

1. Going a little farther, he fell with his face to the ground and prayed, "My Father, if it is possible, may this cup be taken from me. Yet not as I will, but as you will." Matthew 26:39 NIV
2. Page 117, The Practice of The Presence of God, Brother Lawrence, Paraclete Press, 2010 First Printing, The Community of Jesus, Inc.

ABOUT THE AUTHOR

Karen Evans is an author, award-winning photographer, devoted wife, and fur-baby mom. She has a passion for all things written and for The Word, Jesus Christ. She can be found rainforest hiking and seashore strolling with her family and with her camera slung over her shoulder. Karen loves to cook and share delicious food with family and friends. She has travelled extensively throughout the world, and Africa holds a special place in her heart. Karen has written her first book to women with the message of hope, love, and freedom to be found in a relationship with Jesus. Look for a women's fiction novel and a series of children's books from Karen in the near future! Karen lives in the small coastal city of Nanaimo located on Vancouver Island, BC, Canada. She shares her island dream with Steve, her husband of 25 years, and their happy, jumpy dog, Ruby.

Manufactured by Amazon.ca
Bolton, ON

29349004R00120